Contents

I'm OK!

Building Resilience Through Physical Play

Jarrod Green

Redleaf Press®
www.redleafpress.org
800-423-8309

Published by Redleaf Press
10 Yorkton Court
St. Paul, MN 55117
www.redleafpress.org

First edition 2017
Cover design by Amy Fastenau
Cover photograph by Clarissa Leahy / Getty Images / iStock
Interior design by Jim Handrigan
Typeset in Minion Pro
Interior photos by Jarrod Green, except on pages 1 and 2 by Sarajane Dickey and on page 29 by Merryl Gladstone.

Printed in the United States of America
23 22 21 20 19 18 17 16   1 2 3 4 5 6 7 8

Library of Congress Cataloging-in-Publication Data

Names: Green, Jarrod, author.
Title: I'm OK! : building resilience through physical play / Jarrod Green.
Description: First edition. | St. Paul, MN : Redleaf Press, 2017. | Includes
   bibliographical references and index.
Identifiers: LCCN 2016009079 (print) | LCCN 2016020410 (ebook) | ISBN
   9781605544519 (paperback) | ISBN 9781605544526 (ebook)
Subjects: LCSH: Physical education for children. | Resilience (Personality
   trait) in adolescence. | BISAC: EDUCATION / Teaching Methods & Materials /
   General. | SOCIAL SCIENCE / Children's Studies. | EDUCATION / Physical
   Education.
Classification: LCC GV443 .G76 2017 (print) | LCC GV443 (ebook) | DDC
   372.86--dc23
LC record available at https://lccn.loc.gov/2016009079

Printed on acid-free paper

2/18

I'm OK!

Acknowledgments

In both my career and my life I've been surrounded by extraordinary educators who have taught me both explicitly and by their example how to be the teacher I am, and to whom I am deeply indebted.

Thank you to all the wise and generous teachers whose practices have taught me about helping children build resilience and whom I have referenced in this book.

Thank you to all the teachers I've had the privilege to call my colleagues and all the teachers and leaders who have mentored me along the way—to Lisa and everyone at Temple Sinai Preschool; to Belann and Lynn and Saeda and everyone at Pacific Primary; to Barbara and Daniel and everyone at San Francisco State University; to Joan and everyone at Diablo Valley College; to Merryl and Traci and all my truly exceptional colleagues at the Children's Community School.

Thank you to all the enablers and cheerleaders who encouraged me to write—to Gaye; and to Lisa and everyone at Teachers Write Now.

Finally, thank you to my three all-time favorite teachers—to my dad, who taught me that teaching is about writing and communicating and passion and fun; to my mom, who taught me that teaching is about curiosity and creativity and problem-solving and relationships; and to Amelia, who continues to teach me more about teaching, and about resilience, and about life, than she knows.

Introduction

This is a book for early childhood educators who want to connect powerfully and effectively with children's physical learning; who want to meet children's needs concerning physical development, both short and long term; and who see a place for resilience in their goals for children. This book aims to give teachers the tools they need to understand the ideas connected with resilience and strategies for implementing those ideas in their practice. It aims to provide both a theoretical framework and a practical approach for work with children, families, and other educators on resilience. It aims to help teachers not just to build resilience into their own personal approach to teaching but also to create a *culture* of resilience—in their classrooms, in their schools, and in their communities.

Chapter 1 is an exploration of the issues involved in thinking about building resilience in the context of physical play—what the stakes are, why we should care, why we *do* care, and what we're likely to encounter. In chapter 2, we'll explore safety and risk in early childhood education and build a theoretical framework for understanding how resilience is connected to children's other needs. Chapter 3 will discuss practical approaches to working with children—how to help children find the appropriate level of physical risk taking, how to respond productively to risky behaviors, how to use physicality as an opportunity to build skills such as self-regulation and self-help, and how to respond when children get hurt. Chapter 4 will discuss working with families—how to build trusting relationships with families around children's physical development by being an effective communicator. In chapter 5, we'll explore approaches to working with teachers—how to discuss resilience with your colleagues and how to effectively ask teachers to change their practices concerning physical development. Chapter 6 will look at concerns about licensing and liability and how educators can feel confident in their legal position while remaining true to their educational goals and philosophy. The closing reflections in chapter 7 will ask you to identify and commit to your values regarding your work with young children. Appendix A provides an outline to use for a workshop on resilience with families, and appendix B will provide you with further reading and resources on the topics discussed in this book.

Each chapter is studded with sidebars containing reflection questions. So much of this book connects with both our teaching practices and our life experiences that it's important for each reader to see where those connections are. As you read the book, I urge you to pause, at least for a few minutes, at each reflection question to consider your own response to the issues the section has raised. If your school or community is exploring issues of physical development and resilience, the reflection questions can be useful prompts for staff meetings, family discussions, teacher groups, and so on.

While you are of course free to look through this book in any order you choose, or simply to find the sections that seem most valuable or urgent, I urge you to read the chapters in order. You'll find that many of the ideas in this book are the same from section to section and that they acquire deeper layers as we revisit them in new contexts. Similar approaches are effective and appropriate in a surprising variety of situations. For instance, you'll find that a strategy for supporting a child who's nervous about climbing the jungle gym will also work to support a teacher who's nervous about what will happen if she allows children to take physical risks. A strategy that helps you communicate with a parent when a child has been injured will help you communicate with your licensing consultant about the safety of part of your playground. Similar approaches come up again and again because the principles involved are universal. In particular, you'll notice that *building relationships* is a theme throughout the book as a key ingredient in all aspects of your practice.

I hope this book will feel like a blend of new and old—that the principles and philosophies will feel familiar as things you've always known and thought, but that their applications will feel exciting and helpful and give you energy and confidence to make resilience a bigger part of your teaching practice.

Here's to bouncing back!

~ 1 ~

Personal Connections

Our Childhood Experiences

Some of my very earliest memories are of my dad throwing me in the air. When I was one and two years old, my dad would throw me up in the air and catch me, and I would laugh and squeal, "Again! Again!" My favorite part was when he'd wait until I got to knee level before he snatched me out of the air. My mom always worried he'd drop me, but he never did.

When I was five we had an orange tree in my backyard. It had these twisty branches that spread out right from the base and hardly any leaves or twigs until the very ends of the branches, so it was perfect for a small child like me to climb. I could climb up and look down on my family without (I thought) being seen—it was my private little hideaway high above the ground. In retrospect it was probably only about six feet off the ground, but it felt high and dangerous and secret.

One-year-old Jarrod and his father.

Four-year-old Jarrod in his backyard orange tree.

When I was seven we moved to a house up in the Oakland hills where we had a backyard that we called "the ravine," though really it was just a moderately steep hill with bushes and eucalyptus trees. The best thing about it, besides simply being a place to go hang out in that felt wild, was that the ivy would climb up the trees and then hang down from the branches in vines. My friends and I would find an especially steep part of the hill and leap onto the vines and swing out over the bushes below. When I was about nine one of the vines snapped and I fell on my back and got the wind knocked out of me pretty hard. After that we still swung on the vines, but perhaps not quite as freely as before.

Every summer from when I was four until I left for college, my family went to a camp a little north of Yosemite. My favorite thing to do was go on creek walks—I loved to test my balance on the stones, to judge which rocks would be too slippery to stand on and which could hold me, to see how fast I could jump from stone to stone. Sometimes I went with friends, but I preferred going alone; other people always wanted to go too slowly in some places and too fast in others. Once in a while, I'd slip and fall in the creek, and one memorable time I scraped my leg pretty good and the creek water made it look like there was quite a lot of blood; it was scary and painful, but I made the twenty-minute walk back to our cabin okay by myself. A good creek walk is still pretty much my favorite outdoor activity—though now I have a dog to come with me. My eight-year-old self would have been jealous of my thirty-five-year-old self.

On the other hand, I was definitely *not* a physically adventurous child. My little brother—who has grown up to work, incidentally, as a circus acrobat—was the one who had little regard for physical safety. I wasn't the fast kid or the strong kid or the coordinated kid; I was the kid who could mostly manage to keep up. I would play team sports if everyone else was playing, but I would never choose to if given my druthers. I had friends who skateboarded, but I always immediately fell off when I tried. I liked riding my bike, but hills and streets with cars scared me. I liked playing catch but was terrified of getting hit in the nose with a ball. I *hated* getting hurt, so I didn't often take real risks.

Or did I? I don't have many strong memories of injuries, but looking back, I did do some risky things. The biggest injury I remember was from doing something that was hardly risky at all; in second grade I was jumping over a bench that was no more than a foot tall, and which I had jumped over count-less times before, when I caught my toe and landed face-first on the asphalt. I had a bloody lip and a loose tooth that got even looser, and I spent an hour sitting in the principal's office with an ice pack. For the most part, though, I don't really remember the injuries or how I recovered from them. I remember climbing trees, jumping through creeks, and getting tossed in the air.

It's notable to me that adults play a very little role in most of these mem-ories. The physical play that was most important to me, most exciting, and where I learned the most, was play that happened when adults weren't around to interfere.

We all had childhood experiences with physicality, even if all our expe-riences were different. Do you have positive memories of physical play when you were young? Perhaps you enjoyed wrestling with a sibling, playing a team sport, being in a dance class, playing tag at school, riding your bike around the neighborhood, or something else. Think about what physical experiences have stuck with you. How did you feel while you were doing those things? What did you get out of them? And why do you think those are the memories that have stuck with you for so long?

How did you feel about physical play in general? Did you enjoy it, or not so much? Were you a rough-and-tumbler or a sit-on-the-sider? Could you keep up with the fast kids? Were *you* the fast kid? And how did other kids react to your physical efforts—did they support you, discourage you, pressure you? What about adults—what role do they play in your memories of physicality? Did they play with you, ignore you, try to stop you?

Did you ever get seriously hurt? Did you ever break a bone or get a concussion as a result of doing something risky? Or, just as likely, did you ever get hurt while doing something routine, like I did jumping over the bench? How much do you remember about the feeling when you got injured? Do you remember the recovery process? Did it change anything about how you played afterward?

Positive or negative (or, for most of us, mixed), we all had lots of experiences with physicality when we were children. And for better or worse (or again, for most of us, mixed), those experience affect how we interact with the physicality of the children we work with.

Our Adult Experiences

In our culture most of us learn sooner or later that it's not cool to run around and climb trees anymore and that we're either supposed to start playing team sports or stop being physical.[1] I stopped being physical. For middle school, high school, college, and some years after, I rarely did anything that was physically strenuous or adventurous.

That said, as I've aged, I've found more ways to reconnect with physical activity. I still like climbing trees (not that our culture offers adults many socially appropriate opportunities for that) and creek walks. I like to play around with activities like juggling and balancing, and I've taken enjoyable classes in activities such as trapeze and rock climbing. I find that, much to my surprise, I don't hate going to the gym, and I actually feel pretty good

---

1 My little brother, Zach Fischer, the aforementioned circus acrobat, often despairs that our culture more or less teaches children that the only acceptable outlets for physical activities are rule-bound, adversarial team sports, such as baseball, football, or soccer. "A lot of people don't like teams, rules, or winners and losers, so they think they don't like moving their bodies," he says. "But there are physical activities for everyone! Everyone should get a chance to try rock climbing and cross-country skiing and trapeze and tightrope walking and juggling and weight lifting and bicycle racing and karate and a hundred others! People say they don't like to move their bodies before they've tried even a fraction of the options."

after I go. I've taken jobs where being physically confident and coordinated is useful—climbing ladders and lifting heavy equipment when I worked in theater;[2] roughhousing and tossing kids in the air now that I teach preschool. It's taken me years to relearn that I enjoy physical play—something I never doubted when I was five.

I still enjoy, roughly speaking, the same kinds of physical activities as an adult as I did as a child—playful, individual activities that require coordination and risk taking more than endurance or strength. Is that because my positive experiences back then bring positive associations now? Or are my preferences innate, and I like the same kinds of activities now because I'm the same person I was then?

How about you? How do you relate to physicality as an adult? Are you physically active? If so, is it because you enjoy it or because you feel like you're supposed to? (Boy, does our culture make us feel like we're supposed to.) What kinds of physical activities are the most fun for you? The same kinds of things you enjoyed when you were young, or different? Do you do any physical things that feel like play? How do you feel when you do something active?

Adults have as much of a physical life as children do, though it can be easy to pretend we don't. And like it or not, the way we feel about physicality as adults influences how we connect with the physicality of the children we teach.

Our Teaching Experiences

As a teacher of young children, I see a very different side of physicality from the side I saw as a child. Every day at school is a carnival of running, chasing, climbing, jumping, dancing, riding, crashing, spinning, building, falling, laughing. We use our bodies all day every day. And by "we" I of course mean the children and myself. I could let the children do all the physical play, but where would be the fun in that? I like to do that stuff too, and there are all sorts of reasons why my teaching is better when I join in. (See "Relationships and Physical Development" in chapter 3.)

---

2 Before I worked in early childhood, I had a career as a lighting designer and theater technician.

When I was a child, my focus was entirely on the fun aspects of physicality. Now that I'm charged with caring for children, my attention is drawn more to risk and injury. I certainly witness my share of risky physical behavior. Kids run and bike without looking where they're going; they roughhouse at inappropriate times and places; they jump from high places without a safe landing zone; they find all kinds of ways of risking injury to themselves and others. The children at my school are no more and no less physically adventurous, I think, than any other group of three-year-olds anywhere—this is just what young children do. There are plenty of injuries at my school. As in any program for young children, scrapes and bumps and bruises happen regularly, along with shouting and crying. Injuries attract a lot of attention, from children, families, and teachers alike. Serious injuries, however, are extremely uncommon. The vast majority of injuries leave no mark at all and are forgotten within minutes. We've sometimes gone weeks without reaching for the first aid kit. I've found that the attention I pay to the possibility of injuries is sometimes out of proportion to the number and severity of injuries that actually occur.

That's not to say that dealing with injuries isn't important. On the contrary, helping children recover from all kinds of negative experiences—injuries, frustrations, disappointments, conflicts—is a core part of my practice. An injury may not leave a physical mark, but the learning that comes out of it can be invaluable. (See "Responding to Injuries" in chapter 3.)

As I pay attention to my own perspectives on physicality, I notice the extremely wide range of perspectives among the children, families, and colleagues I work with. I've cared for children who need to take a break for half an hour after another child brushes against them, and children who barely notice the most dramatic falls. I've worked with families who need a half-hour conversation about injuries that leave no mark, and families who see a scrape down the length of their child's face and simply smile and say, "You must have been doing something exciting!" I've worked with caring and dedicated colleagues who hover protectively right next to the slide, and caring and dedicated colleagues who calmly watch from several feet away while children hang from the monkey bars by their knees—as well as caring and dedicated colleagues who hang upside down from the monkey bars alongside the kids. I can confidently say I've seen every possible way to approach physical play, safety, risk, and injury with young children.

How about you? What have your experiences as a teacher been around children's physicality? Do you enjoy children's risky play, or does it scare you—or both? Do you play with the children, stay on the side, or try to stop them—or all three at different times? How do you feel when children get hurt? Have you been present for any especially bad injuries? How do you feel about talking to families when children are injured? How do you feel about your colleagues' interactions with children and families concerning these issues?

We all want what's best for children, of course, as well as for families and colleagues. And, like everyone, we're also driven by what's best for ourselves—what makes us feel comfortable, happy, and successful. As you explore the issues in this book—issues of physicality, risk, play, and resilience—you'll be reminded of experiences you've had as a child, as an adult, as a teacher. In fact, I'll be asking you specifically to connect what's in this book with your experiences, because this is personal stuff. If we want to change our practice to best meet children's needs, we'll need to understand our own relationship to the issues in order to be effective.

Physicality and Childhood

Children are physical beings.

In a way, that's almost too obvious to mention. Babies do a lot of looking and touching and feeling and moving; they don't do a whole lot of "thinking," at least not in the same way that adults do. When they're toddlers they move through the world touching everything, moving everything, bumping into everything. When they're in preschool they start to be able to have real conversations, but immediate physical stimuli are more salient than ideas. Even the most intellectual of grade school children can be reduced to weeping or ranting by a stomachache or a bonk on the head. Young children *are* their bodies.

At the same time, children's physicality can be easy for us to forget. As adults we tend to interact primarily in a cognitive way—we have ideas, which we communicate to each other through words, and we expect that others will understand and respond to our ideas with ideas of their own. As early as two years old children start to be able to participate in conversations, and they make it easy to forget, as they turn three and then four, that they are not yet as rational as we are (or as rational as we like to *think* we are) and that they are still experiencing the world more through their senses and bodies than through their developing intellects.

Jean Piaget described the "sensorimotor stage" of cognitive development covering the first two years of life. The infant, in this framework, starts by interacting with the world only through reflexes, but gradually builds up repeated behaviors that get positive reactions from the world, eventually beginning to create mental representations of the world based on those inter-actions. Modern research has complicated much of Piaget's original outline: we now know that even the youngest infants engage in genuine cognition and that children much older than twenty-four months are still interacting with the world in a physical, trial-and-error kind of way. But the basic model is cor-rect for all young children: they take physical actions and observe the result-ing changes in their sensory input, and they use that feedback loop to learn about . . . well, to learn about everything, really. Children's brains are quite lit-erally restructured by the sensory input they receive and the motor impulses they put out. The combination of those two physical experiences allows chil-dren to learn to walk and talk, to tie their shoes and ride bikes, to write their names and have conversations with friends. There's no learning experience that children have that is not a physical interaction with the world.[3]

Learning about physical experiences precedes more abstract learning in all domains. For instance, in cognitive development you have to spend some time picking up blocks and moving them around before you can learn to count them. In emotional development you have to learn that you can recover from your physical feelings (like hunger and pain) before you can learn to recover from emotional feelings (like fear and frustration). Socially, you learn how the physical world responds to you ("I knocked something over and it broke") before you understand how other people respond to you ("I knocked my friend over and she cried"). Physical learning is the basis of all learning.

This process is often most obvious when it goes wrong. I had a three-year-old child in my classroom some years ago that I'll call Jimmy. Jimmy was

---

3   There are any number of other models of children's thinking and learning that don't look through the lens of physical experiences, including Piaget's own descriptions of the later stages of development, which he casts much more in terms of internal mental processes than physical experiences. I feel strongly, however, that there are multiple correct ways to look at children's thinking. Different frames are useful for different purposes, and for our purposes at the moment the physical frame is most useful.

that kid who seemed to be constantly bumping into things and falling down, falling out of his chair, tackling friends, and so on. A colleague remarked, "It's like he doesn't know where his arms and legs are." Jimmy had what is often referred to as sensory processing disorder[4]—he had a hard time coordinating and managing the input from his eyes, ears, skin, and muscles. He had a lot of behaviors that were the direct result of his physical disorganization, such as falling down; he also had a lot of behaviors that were a result of his attempts to manage his disorganization, such as tackling other children to get more sensory input from them. At the start of the year we could already see how Jimmy's physical disorganization was becoming mental disorganization: he had a hard time learning to count because it was hard for him to move his finger from one object to the next in order; he had a hard time having a conversation about any particular idea because a small noise or movement would pull his attention away from what he was talking about. Over the course of the year we watched as his physical and mental disorganization started to build into social disorganization: his random outbursts and falls were funny to other children, so he started acting the part of the class clown. He had a hard time not bashing into other children, so children started treating him like an unpredictable hazard. Jimmy was a sweet, creative, optimistic child, but at three years old he was on his way to long-term challenges in learning and social development because he couldn't depend on his body to interact with the world successfully.[5]

All right, so children are physical creatures who need the right kinds of sensorimotor experiences to grow into the thinking, feeling, interacting beings we want them to be. What kind of experiences do children need exactly?

---

4   Sensory processing disorder (SPD) is not officially diagnosable, since it is not included in the DSM-V; it is, however, included in the Diagnostic Classification of Mental Health and Developmental Disorders of Infancy and Early Childhood (DC:0-3R). Many early childhood professionals find SPD a valuable frame for understanding the needs of "clumsy" and "disorganized" children.

5   Fortunately, late in the year Jimmy started receiving services from an excellent occupational therapist, who gave Jimmy, his family, and his teachers strategies to help him organize his body and his senses. For resources to help support similarly "disorganized" children, see "Sensory Needs" in Appendix B.

- **Sensory input**—All kinds! They need to touch stuff and see stuff and smell stuff and all the rest, with as much variety as possible. Children should pet a rabbit, put a piece of lemon in their mouths, skin their knees, look at art, listen to live music, smell herbs and spices, get squeezed in a bear hug, hang upside down, and have any other kind of sensory experience they can (metaphorically) get their hands on.

- **Opportunities to act on the world**—Remember, it's not just input; it's the feedback between input and output. Children need to do stuff and see what happens, to observe cause and effect in their world. They need to build with blocks and watch them fall down and hear the noise they make; they need to hold something delicate and learn to keep it safe, or find out what happens if they don't keep it safe; they need to jump from someplace a little scary and see how it feels when they land; they need to say something in a conversation and see how people respond. Every action is a little experiment in how the world works.

- **Opportunities for physical activity**—To be good at acting on the world, children need to be good at using their bodies. They need to work their large muscles by running, climbing, jumping, dancing, spinning, swinging, and wrestling. They need to work their small muscles by drawing, touching, taking apart, putting together, breaking, fixing, and feeling. (You may have noticed that when children don't have opportunities to do this stuff, they just go ahead and do it anyway. That's how deep the need is!)

- **Pleasure**—Since their bodies are the route to all future learning, children need to learn that their bodies are awesome to use. If running feels good, they should run a lot. If snuggling in the pillows feels good, they should do that. There are limits to this, of course,[6] but for the most part children need opportunities to learn that their bodies can give them success and fulfill-

> ## REFLECTION
>
> How did your physical experiences as a child—positive or negative—influence who you are? Would you want the children you care for to have physical experiences like the ones you had? Would you want them to get similar things out of their physical experiences as you did?

---

6   I, for example, learned when I was eight that although jelly beans taste delicious, there is such a thing as eating too many of them.

ment and pleasure, so that they'll be able to use their bodies for learning throughout their lives.

Lost . . .

As obvious as it may be that children are physical beings who need a variety of physical experiences in order to develop, as a culture we seem to have a problem letting children have those experiences. Most children in today's culture in the United States experience much less unsupervised play than the children of a few decades ago, especially physical play (Entin 2011). Most children are far more likely to play soccer on an organized team with adult instruction than to play kick-the-can or touch football on the street in their neighborhood. They're more likely to be driven to a playdate than to ride their bikes to a park. They're more likely to be told "It's not safe to play outside alone" than "Don't come home before sundown."

There are a lot of reasons for this cultural shift in how children are expected to spend their time. Partly it's a simple question of opportunity—there are more classes, clubs, and other organized events for children today than there used to be, so more families sign their children up for such activities. Relatedly, as our society has started to realize how important childhood experiences are, families want to give their children the "best" childhood experiences possible, which often means that many families try to organize as many experiences as they can on their children's behalf. There's also a practical, demographic change that's related: as families have become more mobile over the course of their lives and have increasingly moved within and between cities, children are much less likely than they used to be to live within walking distance of friends' houses, so socializing and playing require more adult assistance than before.

But the main reason children have so much less unsupervised play than they used to is fear—we worry about "what could happen" if children are unsupervised. In the name of safety and protection, playgrounds remove teeter-totters and swing sets; schools ban running at recess; children are not allowed to play unsupervised. And as much as we fear for children's safety, we also fear litigation we might be faced with "if something happens," so we remove possible risks, "to be on the safe side."

Relatedly, most people mistakenly believe that crime against children is common, when in fact the reverse is true: nationally, crime rates have been falling steadily for decades; violent crimes have fallen by more than half since the early 1990s (Wolfers 2014). Additionally, crime against children committed by strangers is astonishingly rare (Skenazy 2015). By attending to the very worst incidents, the media make people think violent crimes are common and teach families to be fearful for their children's safety.

Families are also subjected to more judgment of their parenting (both real and perceived) than ever before. The media plays a role here as well: from the thousands of parenting books that say you're doing it wrong to news reports of children being taken away from families who let them walk to the corner store alone, families are made to be very conscious of how their parenting is perceived. They fear not only for their children's safety but also for what people will think of them as parents if something happens.

The result is that the adults who care for children are deathly afraid for children's safety. The lionization of safety leads to oversupervision and the attempt to remove risk from children's lives. And in the name of protecting children from danger, we protect them from developmentally appropriate physical activity as well. Many children don't get to swing on swings, ride on teeter-totters, play with friends in front of their houses, or walk to school.

In no specific instance is this approach incorrect. It's not wrong to drive children to friends' houses for playdates; it's not harmful to sign them up for the soccer team; it won't ruin their lives to remove a swing set from the playground. Together, these actions do result in fewer injuries. But cumulatively, these actions add up to a world in which children don't have the physical experiences they need. A wide variety of sensory input and gross-motor activity, opportunities to act on the world in a physical way, the chance to find joy in the physical world—these are not optional experiences. These are *needs*, and yet our culture removes them from children's lives more and more.

That removal comes at quite a price. Children may have safety, but they've lost the growth that happens from taking risks, the learning that happens from trial and error, the benefits that come with injury. Joy, growth, and learning come from the physical play that is a natural part of childhood—and as a culture we have allowed a lot of it to be lost.

. . . and Found

Fortunately, many people (including you, since you're reading this book) have started to realize that there's a problem—that children are losing out on physicality and are not better off for it. People see the need to help children reconnect to physical play, to help them recover what's been lost.

Many teachers who care about children's physicality have noticed the startling disconnect between the best-practice approaches we use to support children's cognitive, social, emotional, and academic learning and the approaches we take to their physical learning:

- **Constructivism:** This approach says, in part, that children learn through hands-on trial and error and that failure is a crucial component of learning—but in physical development, we fear that the "error" part of trial and error is too dangerous to allow.

- **Social constructivism:** This approach values input, ideas, and collaboration from others as key to learning—but in physical development, we worry that peers will egg each other on toward danger and give each other "bad ideas."

- **Whole-child perspective:** As educators, we are asked in this perspective to attend to the interconnections between all domains of development—but we tend to minimize physical development as children's "blowing off steam" or "getting their wiggles out."

- **Ecological model:** This model sees the environment as an inextricably interconnected part of the child—but we often try to curtail children's instinctive approaches to interacting with their environment: "Don't touch that," "Come down from there," "Please don't run in the classroom," and so on.

- **Strengths-based approach:** In this approach, we are asked to focus on supporting a child's abilities, capacities, skills, and interests, instead of trying to "fix" the things that are "wrong"—but in physical development, we're often asking children to stop doing the very things they feel most excited and confident about.

- **Long-term perspective:** Keeping the long term in mind in cognitive, social, and emotional development helps us see the big picture of how frustration or failure in the short term can be an important and powerful part of development over time—but in physical development, we're often more concerned with preventing injury right now than with building long-term skills.

There are valid reasons why these approaches and perspectives, which are such an accepted part of best practices generally, are hard to apply to physical development. Yet the fact that we know they *are* best practices requires us to try to apply them, even if it's difficult. One way forward is to ask what it is you feel the children you care for are missing—and what it is you want to give to them.

> ### REFLECTION
>
> What is it you want the children you care for to get out of their cognitive, social, and emotional experiences? What are the perspectives or approaches that you use to accomplish those goals?
>
> What is it you want the children you care for to get out of their *physical* experiences? Is there a way to apply the same perspectives and approaches?

Resilience

What I want to give the children in my care is resilience—the ability to bounce back from life's setbacks. Life is full of setbacks, even for children—in fact, *especially* for children. How often do young children face disappointments, frustrations, unpleasant surprises? They have to confront anger, sadness, and fear much more often than most adults. A three-year-old gets more bonks on the head in a day than you get in a year. And when was the last time you experienced the profound disappointment a four-year-old feels when he's not in the art project group he was hoping for? Young children experience setbacks by the cartload, so early childhood is the perfect time to build skills of resilience that will last a lifetime.

Resilience can be a lot of things. It can be working on a jigsaw puzzle even when you're having a difficult time with it. It can be noticing there's no seat at the table you wanted and saying, "Oh well, I'll find another spot." It can be cuddling your teddy bear when your best friend says he doesn't want to play with you. It can be snuggling up to a teacher when reading a scary book or taking deep breaths to calm down when your family says good-bye in the morning.

And, of course, there's physical resilience. Bumping your elbow and saying, "I'm okay!" Hitting your head and getting yourself an ice pack before sitting down to take a break. Psyching yourself up to climb to the top of the jungle gym, even though it makes you nervous. Trying to climb up the slide, slipping down to the bottom, and deciding to try again. You'll notice that these examples sit at the intersection of the physical and the emotional. This book explores the connection between physical development and resilience, and what we can do as teachers to make resilience a focus of physical learning.

Approaching physical development through the lens of resilience has a lot of advantages. First, it acknowledges the reality of children's essential physicality and allows us to enjoy and support their physical development. Second, it helps us deal with our fear for children's safety by acknowledging risks and helping us focus on the learning opportunities therein (more on that in chapter 2). The resilience approach also helps us by incorporating the best-practice principles of early childhood education that otherwise struggle to find their way into physical development—constructivism and social constructivism, the whole-child perspective and the ecological model, a strengths-based approach and long-term focus. Finally, resilience is a learnable set of skills (rather than an inborn quality), which means that it's a *teachable* set of skills. Resilience is something incredibly valuable that we can give to children—a response to all the physicality that our culture it taking from them.

It can be difficult for early childhood educators to enact a focus on resilience. We live in a culture where there's a lot of fear for children, especially concerning their physicality. It can be challenging to communicate about resilience with families, who rightly prize their children's safety, and with other teachers, who rightly feel charged with children's safety. Beyond that, children absorb the attitudes of the adults who care for them, so they often learn very early that fear and anxiety are the appropriate reactions to physicality.

That said, resilience is a crucial part of our teaching practice. If we want children to grow into confident, engaged, fulfilled, happy members of society, they're going to need the skills to pick themselves up, brush themselves off, and bounce back.

~ 2 ~

Safety and Risk

Safety First

You care about children's safety.

That really goes without saying, doesn't it? You are a dedicated educator, so you care about the well-being of the children you teach, and that includes their safety. Beyond that, you are the caregiver for children when their families aren't around—you have literally been entrusted with the safety of the children in your care.

Your education tells you that if children aren't safe, if they don't *feel* safe, they don't learn effectively. Your experience tells you that if families doubt their children's safety, they don't trust the school and don't engage in their children's education. Your emotions tell you that if *you're* not sure of children's safety, you can't devote yourself to their learning.

Children's safety is fundamental to our work. It is the basis, the prerequisite, for everything we care about as educators.

. . . But Not "Safety Only"

Children need safety. But safety isn't *all* they need.

Children also need discovery. They need challenge. They need adventure, joy, surprise, and comfort. They need hands-on learning and trial and error. They need all the variety of experiences that, together, add up to a childhood.

Part of our job as educators and caregivers is to balance children's many needs, to help give them all the experiences they need to grow and learn and thrive. We must attend to children's need for safety, but we must also meet their other needs.

Another way to think about it is to ask, "What's healthy for children?" Unmitigated risk is unhealthy for children, of course; children with no safety don't have very good outcomes. But a complete lack of risk is also unhealthy: you wouldn't expect a child who grows up swaddled in bubble wrap (figuratively) to be well prepared to enter the real world.

The phrase "safety first" is often repeated, and for good reason. But it's easy to allow "safety first" to turn into "safety should be maximized, no matter the cost." And while that conclusion is logical, it does a disservice to children. If we tried to remove every possible source of injury from children's environment, we would create the blandest possible environment, an environment that would offer children no learning.

There's an analogy to be made between physical safety and protection from germs. We've known since the nineteenth century that germs make people sick; the logical conclusion is to keep children away from germs as much as possible. But science is beginning to understand that a complete lack of germs isn't healthy for children either (Mirsky 2011; Specter 2012). Without exposure to germs, our immune systems don't function correctly, which affects long-term health. Some research shows, for instance, that babies who grow up in houses with pets that spend most of their time outside (and who therefore bring germs inside) get sick less often than other children (Khan 2012). The more the relationship between germs and health is investigated, the more connections are found—there's strong evidence that the presence of germs is important to the functioning of everything from digestion to brain development. So even though germs make us sick, complete protection from germs also makes us sick. In the same way, complete protection from risk—letting "safety first" mean "safety only"—prevents children from developing in a healthy way.

In the United Kingdom, the Royal Society for the Prevention of Accidents has spent the last hundred years promoting safety, and even the society doesn't advocate 100 percent removal of risk (RSPA 2015). The organization's 2009 annual review states that "a quest for 'absolute safety' in all areas of life is not feasible and would come at a cost to freedom." Tom Mullarkey, chief executive of the society, has said, "We must try to make life as safe as necessary, not as safe as possible."

Injury and Childhood

Children get hurt. Everyone involved—families, teachers, the children themselves—agrees that we'd rather children didn't get hurt. Wouldn't that be nice? But the truth is, they do.

It can feel strange to talk matter-of-factly about the certainty of children's injuries, as though we don't care about their safety, or we take their well-being lightly. But the opposite is true. Ignoring the reality of injuries is to deny the real world children are living in, and we do children a disservice when we fail to recognize this in our teaching. Some truths about injury and childhood are important to acknowledge:

- **Injury is inevitable.** You cannot prevent every injury. No matter what you do, some children will get hurt. In a particularly dramatic example, I once watched a toddler enter a room that was 100 percent padded, carpeted, and round-edged and get an injury within thirty seconds that required stitches. If you've worked in early childhood long enough, you've seen something like that too. That's not to say there's nothing you can or should do to promote safety. To the contrary, there's a lot you can do to make injuries less frequent and less serious (see chapter 3). But you can't make any environment injury free, and you can't make any child injury free. You got hurt when you were young. So did your parents and your teachers. And so will the kids you care for.

- **Injury is natural.** Since injury is inevitable, it's a good thing that children's bodies are built to recover. Skin regrows, blood clots, bruises heal. Our bodies automatically release pain-killing chemicals and infection-fighting agents. We evolved in a world where injuries happen, so without any special effort at all, our bodies know how to react to injuries. We're literally built for them![1]

- **Injury is important.** Injury is bad, but that doesn't mean there's nothing good about it. There's a lot to be gained from injury that's hard to gain in any other context. When you get hurt, you learn things about your body—what it can and can't do, for instance. You learn things about your mind and your feelings. You learn things about other people. Some of the things you learn are nice ("I got hurt, but it wasn't the end of the world, and things turned out okay"). Some of the things you learn aren't so nice ("I got hurt, and my friends ran away and left me alone"). But good or bad, a lot of the things you learn are important.

We want the children we care for to be safe, of course. But at the same time, we can recognize that sometimes they will get hurt, they will heal, and good things can come out of it.

> **REFLECTION**
>
> Is there a time you've seen a child get injured in a "safe" space? Is there a time you've seen a child get injured but recover gracefully? Is there a time you've seen an injury that resulted in something positive? How do your answers to those questions affect how you think about injury and about safety?

What Is Safety?

There's no single, straightforward answer to the question "What is safety?"

First off, there are degrees of safety. "*Safe*" can sometimes mean "safe enough." For instance, you might feel safe letting your toddler dig with the plastic shovel but not the metal one. Both could hurt someone, but the plastic one feels *safe enough*. For an adult example, consider that most of us feel comfortable driving, even though tens of thousands of Americans die in car accidents every year (National Highway Traffic Safety Administration 2014)—it feels *safe enough* for us to keep doing it. Furthermore, what's safe enough in

---

1   When children get hurt, I like to talk to them about how well their bodies are designed. "Look at that red, healthy blood coming to where your body got cut! That blood will help the cut heal! Isn't that amazing?" "I know, your hands hurt from where they hit the ground. But you know what's cool? Your hands knew just how to save the rest of your body! Your hands caught you so that your face didn't get hurt! Your hands are so smart!"

one context might be too risky in another—you might be comfortable walking to the corner store after dark but won't let your teenager do the same.

Then there are *perceptions* of safety—what seems safe to one person might seem unacceptably risky to another. How many times have you heard someone say, "Oh, come on, it'll be fine"—or been the one to say it? And even though US cities are the safest they've been in decades (Wolfers 2014), few children are allowed to play outside unsupervised for fear of what could happen—in other words, not because it *isn't* safe, but because it doesn't *seem* safe.

Safety, as a concept, is inherently context specific and subjective, so there's no definitive way to say that something is or is not safe.

Even if safety were objective, it wouldn't necessarily help us that much, because safety is only one value among many. Sometimes you might want to let a child do something that's a little unsafe so that he learns about consequences, or because he's exploring an idea that's really interesting and worth investigating, or because he usually has trouble connecting with other children but he's making a friend with this activity. Those decisions will always be judgment calls—best made by responsive caregivers on a case-by-case basis. Whether something is safe is never the only concern.

As with any other value, there are different cultural attitudes and assumptions about safety. Some cultures place a high premium on children's physical well-being. Some value children's autonomy. Some cultures esteem "being tough." Some place a high importance on children experiencing the consequences of their actions. All these values may be held to varying extents by different families, teachers, and staff members with whom you work. Safety is important, but it is not equally important to all people in all contexts.

Safety, then, is a necessarily complicated and high-stakes concept to discuss, especially considering that we're talking about the well-being of children—children we care about personally, no less. But that doesn't mean we shouldn't discuss safety. On the contrary, it's crucial that we talk openly about safety, what safety means, how much value it holds—with the children we work with, their families, and our colleagues and communities.

Personally, I feel children's safety is important but not singularly important—it has to be weighed at all times with the other things we value for children. I also look at safety as a function of supervision, planning, and appropriateness. In other words, *safety* isn't the same as "lack of injury";

REFLECTION

How do you decide what's safe for a child? Can you come up with general rules for safety that apply in all contexts, or do you need something more complicated? Would your answer change if you were trying to explain it to a child? How about to a parent? To another teacher?

rather, it is a proactive, positive quality of an environment, which takes ongoing consideration and work to maintain. A safe school, to me, is a school full of teachers who know the children well and create an environment tailored to their needs on an ongoing basis—which isn't the same as a school where no one gets hurt.

What Is Risk?

Many of the concepts of safety, especially regarding physical development, connect to the idea of *risk*. Young children do all sorts of physically risky things. Take a second to imagine some of them right now: children jumping from places that are way too high, climbing the wrong way up the slide while other children are coming down, climbing up the outside of the climbing structure, swinging sticks, throwing rocks, running in the classroom.

When we see behaviors like these, our hearts stop a little bit. Teachers of young children are caregivers, and we instinctively think, "What if he lands on his head?" or "What if she hits someone in the face?" But if we really want to give children what they need—including experiences of adventure, triumph, and learning, as well as opportunities to build resilience—we need our understanding of risk to go beyond our knee-jerk, protective impulses. Let's talk about risk as a general concept and then talk about risk with regard to young children.

First of all, what even is risk? Most of us think of risk as the chance of something bad happening. If you take a risk on an investment, it means you might lose your money. If you take a risk trying a new food at a restaurant, it means you might hate it. If you take a risk and let someone set you up on a date, it means your date might be a jerk. The part that's easy to forget is that, as much as risk is the chance of something bad happening, it is equally the chance of something good happening. You risk that investment in the hope of making money. You order something new because it might be delicious after all, or at least different. You go on that date because, hey, you never know, right? Risk is the chance of both a negative and a positive outcome.

That makes sense, of course. If risks were only chances for something bad to happen, no one would ever take one. We actually take risks all the time, because very often the chances of something good far outweigh the chances of something bad. The bad outcome might not be all that bad: you might buy a lottery ticket, for instance, because even though you almost certainly won't win, it doesn't cost very much, and you won't be very upset if (when) you lose. You might also take a risk because the bad outcome is unlikely: you drive to work every day, knowing that car accidents happen all the time, because you know it's very unlikely an accident will happen to you personally. We constantly make risk assessments, making everyday choices by weighing the good side (how good is the thing that might happen, and how likely is it?) against the bad (same questions).[2]

Let's apply these concepts to the physical risks children take. Children make choices that could result in something bad happening—hurting themselves, for instance, or hurting someone else. But we must remember that, inherent to the nature of risk, in these situations there is necessarily something *good* that might happen too. That benefit might affect a child's physical development ("I learned to do something new with my body!"), cognitive development ("I figured out how to solve a problem!"), emotional development ("I was scared, but I did it anyway!"), social development ("I played a game with a new friend!")—or, often, all of the above. It is our job as educators to see not just the negative possibilities of a risky behavior but also the always-present positive ones.

Just like an adult's risky behavior, a child's risky behavior is often worthwhile because the possible negative outcome isn't all that bad (a scraped elbow isn't actually that big a deal) or isn't all that likely (it'd be bad if a child fell off the monkey bars onto her head, but that hardly ever happens).

> **REFLECTION**
>
> Think of a specific time you've stopped a child from doing something because "it's not safe." If you had not stopped the child, what's the worst that might have happened? If you had not stopped the child, what's the best that might have happened? How likely was the worst outcome, and how likely was the best?

---

2   There is a vast amount of social science literature detailing how humans are, by and large, astonishingly bad at risk assessment (George 2012, and others). There are all sorts of systematic errors in our thinking that undermine our ability to accurately determine either the likelihood or the magnitude of good and bad possible outcomes in all kinds of situations. We are instinctive but deeply flawed risk assessors.

Children may not be the best judges of these risks, but with our help, they can get better at it (see chapter 3), and the benefits are always there.

Risk and Early Childhood

The preceding section discusses principles of risk that apply equally to children and adults of all ages. But there are some aspects of risk that are particular to early childhood. A friend of mine once remarked, "Preschool is the best place in the world to skin your knee," and he was right for a number of reasons.

First of all, preschool is the perfect *time* for physical risk taking because of children's size. Do you know why humans learn to walk when they're only two feet tall? Because falling two feet doesn't hurt very much! Similarly, when someone who only weighs twenty-five pounds crashes into something, they don't crash nearly as hard as someone bigger. Preschool-age children take a lot of risks, but they're protected from injury (to a degree) simply by virtue of their size. Furthermore, children's bodies heal much faster than adults' (Dillner 2003). Their skin and blood vessels regenerate quickly, and their immune systems are champing at the bit. The bodies of young children are optimized to make the best of falls, scrapes, and bonks. If you're going to take a physical risk, the best time to take it is when you're in preschool.

Second, preschool is the perfect *place* for physical risk taking because you are surrounded by people who are paid to take care of you when you fall. Not just any people, of course, but experts in child development, who are trained in first aid, who care for you as a person, and who are deeply familiar with your personal needs. The only better place in the world for a child to get injured would be in her pediatrician's office. Furthermore, preschools are designed with children's tendency toward injury in mind—corners are padded, climbers have fall zones, and so on. When children do fall, the physical space minimizes the harm. If children are going to take physical risks, the best place to take it is at a preschool.

An awful lot of learning comes with risk taking—learning that is best done when children are young. All obvious and important physical learning aside, a tremendous amount of social and emotional learning comes with physical risks. Children learn what they can and can't do, and how to make good choices for themselves with that information. They also learn to deal with their problems and to make themselves feel better when something goes wrong. In chapter 3, I detail this learning under the rubric of what I call the "self skills": self-knowledge, self-regulation, self-confidence, self-help, and self-comfort.

The learning that comes with risk taking applies to academic development as well. My colleague kindergarten teacher Carrie Fafarman says, "The apprehension children feel when they encounter a word they don't know how to read or an arithmetic problem they don't know how to solve is exactly the same feeling they have when they're standing on top of a big log and don't know if they can jump off. And the confidence they get in successfully jumping off the log makes them more confident in those uncertain moments with reading and math. I talk to parents in my class all the time about how those physical adventures apply to what they more traditionally think of as 'learning.'"

In general, habits are strongly formed in early childhood—especially habits of thinking. Children who take physical risks when they're preschool age have the opportunity to learn that they are strong and capable; that little failures aren't a big deal, and big failures can be dealt with. In short, they'll learn to be resilient. If they acquire this skill when they're young, they'll still have it when they're older. In other words, preschool is the best place in the world to skin your knee.

What Risk Isn't

If risk taking is good for children, we should just always let them do whatever risky thing they want, right? Well, no, of course not. Not all risk is equal, and not all contexts for risk allow for positive learning experiences. Making a few important distinctions will allow the children you care for to get the most out of risk taking:

- **Risk ≠ chaos.** When you say that you allow children to take risks, some people will immediately envision an environment with children hanging from the rafters, throwing objects willy-nilly, crashing into each other, screaming like maniacs. Sounds awful, right? And it would be, because a chaotic environment inhibits learning. Learning happens with organization and reflection, when children have experiences and then have time to absorb what those experiences mean. If the environment is filled with unpredictable sounds, movements, and experiences, children won't be able to learn well. You can and should help children take risks in a *controlled* way, in an environment where they'll have the physical and mental space to consider the outcomes of their actions. ("I'm glad you're all having fun with your adventure climbing! But you're shouting so loudly no one can hear. Can you climb a little more quietly?" Or, "I can see you're enjoying running as fast as you can, but you keep crashing into other children. Can you find a way to run without crashing, or do you need to take a break from running?")

- **Risk to self ≠ risk to others.** If a child chooses to jump from the climbing structure and hurts himself landing, he learns a lot of important stuff about his body and his emotions. If a child is walking next to the climbing structure when all of a sudden someone falls on his head, all he learns is that the world is a dangerous, scary place. A child's action that puts himself at risk helps *him* learn, but his action that puts another child at risk won't help *that child* learn. You can and should allow children do some things that might jeopardize their own safety, but you should disallow behaviors that threaten other children's safety. ("Hold on, someone is underneath you. Don't jump quite yet. Wait until the coast is clear!" Or, "It's fun to throw those rocks in the air and try to catch them, isn't it? But you're throwing them in a place where they might land on other kids accidentally. Where's a place to throw that's far away from other kids?")

- **Risk ≠ foolishness.** A child who carefully considers her ability to jump over a log and falls will learn a lot more than the same child who, distracted and excited, falls over the same log accidentally. The most learning happens with thought and attention. You can't keep children from being silly and distracted, of course, but those are the moments when you might want to stop a behavior before it happens. Similarly, while children usually make pretty good judgments about what they can safely accomplish, you will occasionally see an overconfident child attempt something that could be seriously damaging. Just because you allow some risks doesn't mean you give up your veto power. You can and should let children take risks, but be ready to step in when the child hasn't thought about what he's doing, or when your adult eyes see consequences the child doesn't. ("I see you're excited to jump off the climber, but you're giggling so much I'm not sure you'll be able to do it safely. Take three slow breaths, and then you can jump." Or, "I know you think holding the umbrella will help you fall safely, but *I* don't feel safe watching you do it, so I need you to stop.")

Harm Reduction

If you're not involved in public health, you might not be familiar with the term *harm reduction*—which is a shame, because it's an incredibly useful concept. The idea is that, in general, people will do some risky things no matter what; therefore, instead of ineffectually trying to get them to stop, it's more helpful to arrange things so that when the risks turn out badly, they won't turn out *so* badly.

There are lots of examples from the adult world. The canonical example is giving away free condoms to college students. College students are going to have sex no matter what, and sometimes sex leads to sexually transmitted infections—but if we give them free condoms, there will be fewer STIs. Another example is seat belt laws. People are going to drive in cars, and some car rides will result in accidents—but if we make people wear seat belts, those accidents will result in fewer serious injuries. These programs don't make any attempt to reduce sexual activity or driving; rather, they work to make negative outcomes less likely (condoms) or less severe (seat belts). These particular programs, incidentally, have proved shockingly effective at reducing the negative consequences that can result from these risky behaviors: deaths from car accidents have fallen dramatically since the advent of seat belt laws, and colleges that distribute free condoms see a marked decrease in the prevalence of STIs (Wald 2003; Centers for Disease Control and Prevention 2015).

There are common harm-reduction strategies already in place at many preschools. For instance, choking is always a risk with young children, but the rule "Sit down while you eat" makes choking less likely. Block towers will always be at risk of falling on people, but the rule "Only build as high as your head" keeps blocks from getting so high that they'd be dangerous. Kids will always be in danger of falling off monkey bars and bikes, but we put mulch under the monkey bars and insist on bike helmets so that the falls will be less harmful.

We can expand our use of harm-reduction strategies to help children get the maximum benefits from the risks they choose to take while reducing the danger. Here are some principles to guide you:

- **Prevent foolish risks.** As discussed earlier, allowing risk taking doesn't mean "anything goes." Use your best judgment to stop behaviors when you think they're too much. Moreover, help children to use their own best judgment by asking them to stop and consider what they're doing (see the discussion of "least restrictive action" under "Intervening in Risky Behavior" in chapter 3).

- **Provide appropriate risks.** Children will always find risks to take, so make sure there are risks available that meet children's needs in a context you feel is safe. Find ways for them to experience the sensations of height and velocity and impact that don't risk permanent damage (see "Calibrating Risk for Different Children" in chapter 3).

- **Allow natural barriers.** Allowing children to take risks doesn't mean you have to help them take bigger risks. Let the world create barriers that will help keep children safe. For instance, if a child wants to climb something high but can't get there himself, he may ask you to lift him up—but if you lift him, you'll be putting him in a place he might not be able to safely get down from. Similarly, if you agree to lift a child down from a high place, he'll learn that it's okay to put himself into unsafe situations, because you'll save him; if you coach him in climbing down instead, he'll be able to make more careful choices next time. If he can climb up himself, he can climb down himself (with your encouragement in both directions, of course—see the discussion of self-help in "Building the Self Skills" in chapter 3).

- **Supervise risk taking.** Most important of all, allowing risk doesn't mean a laissez-faire, anything-goes-at-recess approach to physical play. On the contrary, supervision is key to helping children get the most out of risk taking. Supervision gives any number of opportunities to support children's risk taking by maximizing the benefit and reducing the harm—from reducing the danger to others ("If you want to swing that stick, go over to that side where there are no kids who might get hit") to encouraging good choice making ("Last time you built the big blocks that high, I remember they fell on your foot. How will you make sure that doesn't happen this time?"), and everything in between. Supervision is at the core of the ways we can help children to build resilience and will be covered in more depth throughout chapter 3.

A fun physical risk: children jump and try to catch a ribbon I hold just out of reach.

REFLECTION

Think of a time you've seen a child take a risk and succeed. What did the child learn in that moment?

Think of a time you've seen a child take a risk and fail. What did the child learn in that moment?

Children as Risk Takers: What's Realistic?

Many of us think that if we let children do whatever they want, things would quickly dissolve into chaos. We have visions that if we allow risk taking there will soon be children throwing rocks from trees, screaming and chasing each other with sticks, stripped to the waist and covered in paint.

In a way, there is truth to this fear. Young children usually aren't very good at creating organization on their own, controlling their impulses, or making choices based on things other than immediate desires and emotions. But the vision of children as unrestrained, risk-seeking monsters also owes something to our nation's authoritarian culture and the idea (harking back to our Puritan beginnings) that we are born as wild, hedonistic sinners, and only the power of harsh, restrictive rules will make us be good.

But while it is true that children are often bad at creating organization, it is equally true that children need and crave safety and order. The behaviors that look to one person like proof of children's innate wildness another person might accurately label as "boundary-seeking behaviors"—evidence that children want to be contained.

The tension between these views has been explored at Sabot at Stony Point, a preschool–middle school in Richmond, Virginia, that started a practice over a decade ago of letting children spend time in the forest. Preschool teacher Nancy Sowder recalls, "At the start, we had such fear that the children would run every which way in the forest without boundaries. In the playground, children sometimes get pretty revved up. But in the playground, the boundaries are fences, so children don't have to *think* about them. In the forest, it turned out, because there are no physical boundaries, the children are very careful and attend very well. Kids have a very good sense of their own limits. Each new group starting forest practice stays very close to the teachers and moves very slowly until they get more comfortable." Other teachers at Sabot described how being in wild spaces actually brings out qualities of kindness, tenderness, patience, and care in the children. For instance, one day when a child got hurt and there was no ice pack, other children retrieved a rock from the cool stream; "the medicine rock" became a part of that class's culture that year, and children routinely used it to care for one another. The teachers at Sabot discovered that in this wild, risky space, children became much more attentive to safety and caretaking.[3]

We fear that without strict limits preschools will turn into something out of *Lord of the Flies*, but in most cases children are capable of calibrating their behavior to the situation and choosing appropriate risks without adults telling

---

3   There'll be much more about Sabot at Stony Point school and their journey in creating the "forest" practice in chapter 5.

them what to do. Teachers have an important role to play in helping children learn from physical experiences, which we'll explore in depth in chapter 3. But our nightmare risk scenario isn't very realistic. If you assume children will mostly be okay interacting with risk, you'll mostly be right.

~ 3 ~

Working with Children

You care about children's well-being. Of course you do: you're a caregiver! You want children—the children you work with, and children in general—to be healthy and safe, to learn and develop, to be joyful in the world. We've talked about the importance of physical exploration and play, of adventure and challenge, of risk taking and even injury. It's time to explore some concrete strategies. How can a thoughtful educator make sure children get the most out of physical play? How can we talk to them about the risks they take? And what the heck are we supposed to do while they're hanging from the monkey bars?[1]

Create an Environment for Joy and Learning

You're in luck: the first part of your job is pretty straightforward. If children need exploration, challenge, adventure, and risk, then you need to give them an environment where they can get those things. Actually, you're in double luck, because young children are exploration machines; they will find opportunities to invent, discover, challenge, and create in any environment. That said, you can set up your environment to provide *more* opportunities for joy and learning in the physical world.

It's easiest and most natural to create opportunities for physicality outdoors or in a gym (if your program is lucky enough to have one). But remember, young children are physical creatures *all the time*, not just when they go

---

1 What about children with varying abilities? The section titled "Chapter Postscript: Working with Children with Disabilities" at the end of this chapter provides ideas on how to encourage risk taking that includes everyone.

outside. As you read the following suggestions, think about ways you could apply them inside your classroom as well as outdoors.

Opportunities to Build and Create

Open-ended materials that allow children to use their imaginations and explore new ideas are crucial for learning. For physical play, children need to be able to build things that engage their bodies. The following materials encourage children to come up with their own physical activities and adventures:

- **Big blocks:** Expensive big blocks are already a standby for a reason—they can be used to build castles, cars, and creatures that children can actually climb on.

- **Milk crates:** For a cheaper alternative, consider milk crates, which are light but sturdy, and completely weatherproof. Milk crates work best when you have at least a few dozen, so enlist families in searching thrift stores, basements, and yard sales (as well as the curbs and alleys on trash day!).

- **Wooden boards:** These are endlessly useful for building bridges, slides, and ramps.

- **Rope:** A collection of various lengths and types will never be wasted.

- **Big cardboard boxes:** While not structurally sound, big boxes encourage children to interact with physical space in new and exciting ways as they create hiding places, tunnels, houses, and so on.

- **Old tires:** They can be used in a wide variety of ways, and since they roll, industrious children can move them into new configurations without help.

Natural Materials

Objects from nature are some of the best open-ended materials. There's no right way to use them, but there are a million ways they *can* be used, so children are inspired to use their bodies in new ways. Their irregularity encourages problem solving and creativity, and their heft forces children to use their muscles and develop their coordination.

- **Logs and stumps:** These are terrific, since they can be used for building and climbing, and they work great both outdoors and in classrooms. When you see someone in your neighborhood cutting down a tree, ask if you can take some pieces to your school—people usually say yes.

- **Large stones:** They are versatile and will stand up to years of heavy use.

- **Branches and sticks:** What child can resist their allure? Long, hefty branches are great for building, and they aren't very likely to get swung into passersby.

- **Sand, gravel, mulch, and dirt:** These are staples of the preschool yard because of the variety of physical activities they inspire—they can be used for building, art, decoration, storytelling, and so much more!

- **Water:** Nothing compares to its versatile magic—buckets of water, water spouts, hoses, streams, spray bottles, tubes, canals . . . the play possibilities are endless. And of course, these natural materials belong in the classroom as much as outside the school.

Combining Materials

As teachers, we often discourage children from combining materials. "Don't take the blocks on the climber." "Keep the buckets of water away from the swings." "We don't pour sand down the slide." There are good reasons for this, of course—some of the combinations are dangerous, and others will simply be a pain to clean up.

But combinations also inspire new ideas, so be on the lookout for opportunities to mix and match. Take the dress-up clothes over to the big blocks. Tie a rope to the climber. Create a book area underneath the slide. This can work especially well when you combine natural and manufactured materials: try putting the water table in the middle of the milk crates, for instance, or covering the top of the climber with leafy branches. Combinations invite children to see the physical world in new ways, and often encourage children to try new things. A child with no interest in art in the classroom, for instance, may try painting when easel paper is taped to the sidewalk or spread on the ground under a tree. And the next time you see a child combining materials, weigh the gains in joy and creativity against the inconvenience of cleanup before you tell her to stop.

Graduated Challenges

One of the most important qualities of a physical environment, which allows children to continually find joy and learning, is a variety of challenges. Challenges are fun and interesting and offer opportunities to learn, so children naturally seek them out. If appropriate challenges are not available, children will create their own. Do the five-year-olds at your school play in inappropriate ways on the climber? Perhaps the climber's sanctioned uses no longer offer them the challenges they need. Are the two-year-olds trying stunts too dangerous for them? Perhaps there aren't enough challenges pitched at a two-year-old level. Just as your classroom needs a variety of books to keep different levels of readers engaged and a variety of puzzles to keep different levels of puzzle doers busy, your gross-motor spaces need a variety of challenges to keep up with the needs of different children.

Most programs don't have the resources to buy or build different climbing structures for each age group, of course, so you may have to be creative if you want to keep physically adventurous children interested. The open-ended materials mentioned earlier will come in handy. Build a rope swing or an obstacle course. Better yet, invite the children to help you build a rope swing or an obstacle course. If given the chance, children will create and select challenges that are appropriate to their own level of development. It's your job to make sure those options are available.

These are just a handful of strategies for creating an environment of physical joy and learning—a crucial part of fostering healthy children. For resources on creating engaging physical environments for learning, see appendix B.

REFLECTION

Think about the physical environment at your facility. Where do the children already find joy and learning in a physical way? How can you tell? What parts of the environment aren't providing much joy or learning? Can you think of affordable ways to update those areas to better meet the children's needs?

Calibrating Risk for Different Children

As discussed in chapter 2, taking risks is good for children. Risk, by definition, always carries the probability of positive outcomes, and even when a risk goes badly there's still a lot of learning to be had. But of course, "risk is good" is only true to a point, and "all risk all the time" would be a recipe for disaster. The trick is to find the optimal level of risk for each child—enough risk so that there's lots of learning, but not enough to make it likely something really bad will happen.

But how do you get the kids themselves on board? Some take too many risks; some take too few. How do you help them calibrate the right amount of risk? Tom Hobson, a preschool teacher who writes online under the moniker "Teacher Tom," talks to the children at his school about the right number of "bloody owies" (e.g., scrapes and scabs). "If you have no bloody owies," he says, "then you are being too careful. If you have three or more bloody owies then you're not being careful enough. The right number of bloody owies is one or two. That means you're not being too careful or too careless" (Hobson 2014).

That approach may or may not work for you, but the general sentiment— that some kids should take fewer risks than they do, and some kids should take more—is important. Here are some tips to help different kinds of children calibrate their risk taking.

The Bold Child

The bold child takes too many risks. You know who I mean. You're thinking of one of them right now, and imagining his face as he jumps, gleefully and heedless of the danger, from the very top of the climber.[2] He'd jump off the roof if he could just figure out how to get up there, right? The bold child is unafraid of physical risks and doesn't seem to learn from all the risks he takes—and he sometimes endangers other children with his risk taking! The goal is to help the bold child look before he leaps, be able to assess possible consequences, and recognize his own limits.

2　The way we socialize children around gender in our society means that, yes, the bold child is often a boy.

Most of the rest of this chapter is about how teachers can respond to risky behaviors; for the moment I'll just say that adults' responses can help children to reflect on risks, both in the moment and after the fact.

The Cautious Child

You know the cautious child as well—the child who's *interested* in physical activity but afraid to actually participate. She watches from the side as child after child zips down the slide, but she never gets in line herself. She trails after a raucous game of tag but never lets the other children know that she wants to play. She runs up close to the balloon fight but then runs away again immediately. The goal for the cautious child is to build her confidence in her own abilities, especially her ability to keep herself safe, and to reduce her fear of injuries, so that she can get involved in some of the learning experiences she seeks.

One strategy is simply to encourage this child, especially when she finds herself in a little deeper than she expects. I had a child in my class last year I'll call Carol, who repeatedly went three steps up the ladder to the tiny slide before backing down. One day she managed to get one leg over the top of the slide and suddenly was terrified. She yelled for me to lift her down, but I said, "Carol, I will not let you fall. But you did such an amazing job climbing up, I know you can climb back down." After a few minutes of encouragement, along with some explicit instruction ("Now put this hand over here"), Carol got her leg back around and came down. "Wow, Carol!" I said, "You really know how to take care of yourself, don't you? You got yourself back down. That must feel really good." She smiled—and immediately started climbing again.

Another strategy for the cautious child is to provide gentle entries into activities of interest. The presence of a teacher can be enough to make her feel comfortable; you can gradually withdraw later, when the child feels more confident. In a balloon fight, for instance, you might say, "You can stand behind me and hand me balloons to throw." In a tag game you might say, "How about you run right next to me?" When I wrestle with children, I make it clear that the boundaries of the game are the edge of the wrestling mat, and if children want to stop they can just step off the mat. Many children stand right at the edge watching, or quickly step in and then retreat, as a way to feel safe and in control before fully participating.

The Avoidant Child

The avoidant child is uncomfortable with all this running around and crashing. He stays as far away from rowdy games as he can and plants himself in the quietest, safest corner of the gym. In your head he speaks in your grandfather's voice, saying, "I don't want any part of this nonsense! You kids get off my lawn!" The goal for the avoidant child is to build comfort in the world of physical play.

One strategy is to find less-scary and less sensory-stimulating opportunities to explore physical play. The noise and movement in a busy yard can be overwhelming to some children. Small groups can be a great strategy—when everyone else is in the classroom, take five or six carefully chosen kids to the yard to build an obstacle course, or try climbing the ladder when there's no one running or shouting. Providing physical play in different contexts is important as well; a child who won't climb up the slide in the yard, for instance, might climb up a ladder to the reading loft in the classroom.

Another approach is to help the avoidant child build connections to other children. If he has friends in the classroom, he'll be more interested in playing with those same children on the playground. If he feels connected to other children, he'll watch and see when they play happily and safely.

It's important not to pressure the avoidant child into participating where he feels uncomfortable—that strategy will backfire. If you're telling him to play a game where he feels unsafe, not only will he distrust the game, he'll start to distrust *you*—and as we'll discuss later in this chapter, trusting relationships are at the heart of building resilience. Rather than pressuring the child, simply continue to offer safe, engaging, welcoming opportunities to participate, and believe that he'll engage when he's ready.

The Uninterested Child

This child isn't afraid of physical activity—she just couldn't care less. While other children are running and jumping and crashing, she's building with blocks or drawing pictures or playing a not-very-active pretend game. It's not that she won't take risks; she just doesn't see the point. The goal for the uninterested child is simply to build interest in physical play.

The strategy here is to offer more points of connection, more ways to engage with physical play. One way is to offer more variety. Is all your physical play in the playground? Find ways to do some in the classroom, or take a walk to a park. Is all the physical play of the running/crashing/jumping variety? Offer some swings, team sports, or wrestling. Is the only time for active play from 10:00 a.m. to 11:00 a.m.? See what happens when you make time for physicality right at drop-off, or after lunch. A child who doesn't engage with physical play of one type in one context might engage if you vary things.

You can deepen this approach by offering physical play that specifically connects to the interests of the particular child. Does she love to draw? Set up the monkey bars so kids can hang upside down and draw on the ground. Does she like to dress up? Put the dress-up clothes in the tree house. Does she love dogs? Set up a "dog race" in the yard. The more you can connect physical activity to existing interests, the more likely she is to engage.

汉汉汉汉汉汉汉汉汉汉汉汉汉汉汉汉汉汉汉

The caveat is that every child is all of these children—bold, cautious, avoidant, uninterested—at different times. Every child is sometimes gung-ho and sometimes nervous, sometimes scared and sometimes uninterested. The relative proportions might change over time, but these tendencies exist within all children. Which means that all of these strategies are appropriate for all children some of the time. Give the bold child some physical activities tailored to his interests. Give the avoidant child some coaching on thinking ahead. Help the cautious child connect with other children. Set up some easy-to-enter activities where the uninterested child is playing. Sometimes the "wrong" approach for a child will bear surprising fruits. Give it a try. Take a risk.

Responding to Risky Behaviors

Let's say, for the moment, that you've done all the things recommended up to this point. You've gotten your head around the benefits of risk, you've prepared a supportive environment for risk taking, and you've helped all the children you care for achieve the appropriate degree of risk-taking play. Now you're outside, watching the children play, and you see a child doing something risky—climbing on the outside of the climber, jumping off the top of the monkey bars, throwing and catching a pinecone. You want the child to be able to take some risks, but you also want to minimize the harm the child might experience and maximize the benefits from the risk. What do you do, right then in that moment? There are four steps you can take that will help you find a balance between risk and safety. And they only take a few seconds!

Step 1. Trust

Remind yourself that you've given the children a variety of risks to choose from and that the child in front of you is probably choosing an appropriate level of risk for herself. Remind yourself that, to a large degree, children know their own needs and can make good choices. Remind yourself that even if the worst happens—she falls off the climber, say, or the pinecone hits her on the head—permanent damage is extremely unlikely. Remind yourself that the kids doing the craziest physical feats are almost always the most physically competent kids and that "the worst" is unlikely to happen. In short, take a moment to *trust the child*.

Step 2. Observe

Your gut is shouting, "Protect that child!" But does your gut really know what's going on? Reserve judgment for a few seconds and use that time to take in some details about what's going on. It can be dangerous to drop toys off the top of the slide, yes, but is anyone actually underneath who will get hurt? It would hurt to fall from the top of the monkey bars, yes, but does the child actually seem likely to tumble? Watch the child carefully; look at what she's doing, and what's going on in the nearby environment. A few seconds of observation will help you make the best decision.

Step 3. Evaluate

You've observed what's going on, and nothing bad has happened yet. You can spare a few more seconds for some critical thinking. Remember that risk always carries the chance of both negative and positive outcomes—so consider both possibilities. If the worst should happen, how bad would it really be? And how likely is that bad outcome? Remember that "the worst" outcomes we imagine—the concussions, the broken bones—are actually extremely rare and that the vast majority of preschool injuries are quite minor. Often the realistic worst is "she might bump her head"—far from the end of the world. On the other hand, what are the possible positive outcomes of what the child is doing? What could she learn about herself, about the world? What skills could she develop? Remember too that bumps on the head aren't entirely bad—there's a lot of learning to be done by bumping your head. Evaluating the positive sides of the behavior will let you weigh it against the negative side.

Step 4. Act

It's been a good ten seconds now. Your gut reaction has passed, and you've considered things in terms of the child's needs. You can now reasonably choose what action to take—if any. Nothing bad has happened yet—maybe nothing bad will. You can always stay close and keep watching and decide to act later if the situation changes. Or you can choose to intervene, with anything from "I'm going to stand close in case you slip" to "I'm sorry, but that's not safe, and I have to stop you."

When you take the time to go through the four steps, you'll find that you allow children to take more risks. Good! Risk is healthy and positive. You're already helping children learn. But more than that, you'll find that *you* feel less afraid of the risks you see. You're giving yourself practice in reacting calmly to risk and building up your mental library of times you saw kids do risky things that didn't end in disaster. Both children and teachers experience the benefits of risky play when teachers go through these steps.

Here's an example from my practice of following these steps. Some years ago, a class of two- and three-year-olds I was teaching experienced a sudden vogue for climbing up the slide. In the course of a week, we went from seeing only an occasional attempt at summiting Mount Slippery, to seeing many children try it, to seeing multiple children trying to climb up simultaneously throughout our time outside. The slide in question was a good five feet tall, plastic, with a curve halfway down, and fairly slippery. Our heads filled with visions of two-year-olds hurtling over the sides and falling five feet, perhaps bursting into flames upon landing like so many race cars driven off the tracks. Our instinct was to say, "No, you have to stop. That's not safe."

Instead we decided to take the time to observe before responding with a new rule. The teachers gathered in the vicinity of the slide to watch how the children played. We noticed that some of the children could climb all the way to the top, and others couldn't. And yes, some of the ones who couldn't climb it would slip onto their bellies and slide down to the bottom, sometimes taking another child or two down with them. We also noticed, however, that while there were sometimes cries of frustration when this happened, there weren't many cries of pain. No one was falling off the slide, and we realized that the sides were high enough that a child would really have to try to fall off. The kids who slipped to the bottom? Though they might have been frustrated, we noticed most of them would get back up and try again immediately. What persistence! When children were climbing together, they were often laughing with one another and taking pleasure in their shared interests—a level of social connection that was a big deal for some of these twos. And the children who made it to the top? Well, you can only imagine the looks of pride and delight on their faces. Realizing that the benefits of this play were obvious and the risks didn't seem so serious after all, we decided not to address the issue directly with the children but instead simply made sure a teacher stayed close by whenever children were playing on the slide.

A few weeks later the situation changed. The four-year-olds' class schedule shifted, and all of a sudden those kids were sharing some of our yard time. Compared to the twos, the fours were big, heavy, and fast. And boy, did they love running up to the top of the slide and whipping down it as fast as possible! Within two days we'd dealt with half a dozen scared and injured two-year-olds who'd been plowed down the slide by their older counterparts. Even in the face of the obvious problem we still wanted to take a thoughtful approach. We reminded ourselves that nothing *too* bad was happening; indeed, there had been a cluster of injuries, but they had all been minor bonks, nothing even requiring an accident report. We took a little time to watch carefully, and in this case, our instinctual observation was exactly correct: the big kids were knocking down the little ones, who were getting hurt and scared. But we still took the time to evaluate the situation: what were the benefits of climbing up the slide? We had already been seeing those for weeks. And the children clearly loved going down the slide as well. Did we have to ban this play, or was there an action we could take that would minimize the harm and maximize the benefits? We chose to start coaching the children in both classes in the concept of "look before you leap"—a teacher near the slide (who was there anyway) would tell kids at the top, "Check the slide before you go down!" Kids at the bottom would hear, "Look up before you start climbing!" After a couple of days, most of the children had gotten the message and could avoid crashes; teachers quickly gained a sense of which children had a harder time looking out and could focus more energy on coaching those children in keeping themselves and others safe. Both uses of the slide could continue, and the children learned a valuable approach to taking care of themselves and others.[3]

In both stages of this climbing-up-the-slide exploration, my colleagues and I saw behaviors that could have been quite dangerous, and our guts said, "Stop!" But instead of instinctively shutting those behaviors down, we carefully considered how we wanted to react, and the children reaped the benefits of that approach.

Intervening in Risky Behavior

The four steps tell you to trust that children will probably be okay long enough for you to observe their behavior carefully before deciding how to act. But when you decide that action is necessary, what action should it be?

In general, the answer is *the least restrictive action you can take.*[4] If at all possible, you shouldn't control the child or make choices for him, because those actions inhibit the learning you want to promote. Imagine a child is doing something quite dangerous that needs intervention—say, throwing rocks straight up in the air as high as he can. You could stop the behavior by

---

3   For some other wonderful examples of applying the principles of the Four Steps, see Laurie Cornelius's anecdote in *Reflecting Children's Lives*, by Deb Curtis and Margie Carter (Redleaf 2011, pages 55–64). Cornelius tells the story of her experience as a preschool director in Vancouver dealing with a brand-new outdoor play space, which offered many new challenges for children, and how the teachers responded to unexpected new risks in the children's behaviors.

4   If this phrase reminds you of the "least restrictive environment" principle used in special education, that makes sense. Both principles are based on the value of giving children the opportunity to learn and develop in the most open, self-guided way possible.

taking the rocks away or saying, "Stop that—it's not safe," but what would the child learn? The lesson he learns might be "If something gets too dangerous, someone else will stop it for me." Or, "If I want to do anything interesting, I'd better do it when adults aren't looking." Or, "Things that feel fun and exciting to me are actually wrong and bad." All of these lessons would be the opposite of the healthy, productive messages we want to promote.

What we want is for the child to make active, well-considered choices about physical play, so that he has the most opportunity to learn from his experiences. Sometimes it's best simply to *provide information*: "Those rocks are coming very close to your head," or "It hurts when rocks fall on people." For many children, that little piece of perspective will call attention to the choice they're making and get them to change their behavior.

Of course, the child who is likely to throw rocks in the air may not be the child who is likely to respond to elliptical hints, so it can help to engage directly in some dialogue. You can *encourage memory*: "Yesterday you were throwing rocks in the air too. Do you remember what happened?" This strategy not only helps the child draw on his own experiences to make decisions, it also engages him in two-way communication, which supports conscious decision making. Similarly, you can *encourage foresight*: "What do think would happen if you didn't catch one?" Imagining possible consequences is a skill that takes time to develop, but scaffolding from an adult can help a child make thoughtful different decisions by utilizing this growing capacity.

Of course, some children, in the face of these strategies, will keep right on doing what they're doing. *And that's okay.* They've made an active, conscious choice about their own bodies[5] and are therefore better prepared to deal with the consequences. If it works out poorly (see "Responding to Injuries" later in this chapter), you can resist the temptation to say, "I told you so." They already know you told them so, and if you don't rub it in their faces they'll be more apt to listen next time when you encourage them to reflect on their own experiences. If it works out well, you can swallow your pride and tell the child, "I'm sure glad that rock didn't hit you on the head. I was worried."

---

5   Remember from chapter 2 that it's a different story if a child's behavior is endangering *other* children. I might tell this particular child, "Those rocks might land on someone else. If you want to throw them, I need you to find a place far away from other children."

My friend Carrie Fafarman teaches kindergarten at the Philadelphia School, where the teachers take the children to play and learn in the woods once a week for a few hours. As you can imagine, all kinds of opportunities to learn from risky behaviors come up. One of Carrie's strategies is to encourage reflection and self-knowledge. For instance, if a child is about to attempt a risky leap off a log, Carrie might ask, "If you fall down, will it ruin your day?" Some children aren't bothered by a few bumps and can make the informed decision to risk it. Other children reflect that a bruise will leave them crying for an hour, and they decide it's too big a risk to take. Still others use the opportunity to take extra precautions against falling. Carrie finds that thinking about the possible consequences encourages most children to give it a try, knowing the downside won't be too terrible. When children make conscious, deliberate decisions about risk taking, they're more likely to feel good about the outcome—*whether the outcome is good or bad*. Children run up to Carrie throughout the day and say things like, "Look at this bruise I got—I know how to do the jump better next time" or "I got scratched by the prickly bush, but it was in my comfort zone!"

What it comes down to—all four steps for responding to risky behaviors, all the strategies for intervening—is trusting children. Trust is step 1, but it really encompasses all the steps. You trust children to be okay, whether or not a particular behavior works out well. You trust them to make reasonable decisions when they have the opportunity. You trust them to know their own needs and to have ideas that are worth pursuing. You trust them to take care of themselves long enough for you to consider your response.

Reflecting on Risky Behaviors

However much you trust children, their risky behaviors will always give you cause for reflection. You'll stop a child from jumping from a high place but then wonder if your intervention was necessary. A child will get hurt on the monkey bars, and you'll wonder if you should have known to step in. A child will throw pinecones in the air, and you won't be able to decide whether to act or not. You'll always have questions, and that's okay. It's the nature of caring for children. But when you're wondering, it helps to have a thought process to go through. The following questions may help you sort through your thoughts. They can be used to reflect on any behavior, but are particularly useful around risky behaviors.[6]

- **What details of the behavior stand out?** Articulate for yourself the things you noticed about the behavior. What exactly was the child doing? Where did it happen? Who else was around? What about the behavior particularly caught your attention?

- **What are the child's strengths?** Help yourself trust the child by articulating her competencies. What physical skills was the child showing in the behavior? What physical skills has she shown in similar situations in the past? What are her relevant cognitive, emotional, and social strengths?

- **What is the child's point of view?** There's always something worthwhile in the child's perspective. How did she see the situation? How did she feel about it? What was she trying to accomplish?

- **What is influencing the child's behavior?** Lots of things influence children's behavior; you can better support children by understanding those influences. What is the physical environment "telling" the child to do? What are peers telling the child to do (verbally or nonverbally)? How are teachers' actions—including yours—affecting the child's behavior? What in the child's background and experiences might be affecting the child's behavior? (For instance, what response does this behavior get at home?) Is the child being influenced by the media? (For instance, is she acting out a story from a book or a TV show?)

- **What is influencing my response?** Support the child more fully by examining your own reactions and perspectives. How do you feel about what you see? What experiences are contributing to that feeling? Does this behavior remind you of teaching experiences you've had? How about experiences from your childhood?

- **What theories are relevant?** Bring your broader educational approach to bear on this situation. Could you look at this situation through a constructivist lens? Is the "whole child" model relevant here? Are there

---

6 These questions were adapted from *Learning Together with Young Children*, by Margie Carter and Deb Curtis (Saint Paul, MN: Redleaf, 2008).

opportunities for social development or academic learning in this situation that you should take advantage of?

- **What values should inform my response?** Think about the big picture of what you want for children, and let that color your thinking. What are the qualities you want to build in the children you care for? Thoughtfulness? Creativity? Kindness? Independence? Joy? Resilience? How could this moment be an opportunity to build these qualities?

Reflecting on the preceding questions can help you see the child and her behavior in a broader, better-considered light and inform the way you respond to behaviors, the way you teach. Of course, it'll almost always be impossible to consider these questions in the moment when you're looking at a behavior. When children are running-climbing-jumping-chasing-crashing, it's a challenge to take even the ten seconds to go through the Four Steps, let alone do some deep introspection. These questions are a better tool to use after the fact, when you have a moment to think. At the end of the day, when you're putting away the playdough and something you saw comes to mind, pull out these questions and mull them over. When you're writing in your teaching journal at home, use these questions to frame your thoughts. When you're in a team meeting, use these questions to guide a conversation about the children and their play.

The more you get used to rolling these questions around in your mind, the more they'll inform your thinking throughout the day. You won't have to go through them all in a moment of decision, but they'll already be in your head, helping you sort through what you're seeing. Building a habit of reflecting on children's behaviors helps you teach all the time, even when you're not actively reflecting.

REFLECTION

Think of a specific risky behavior you've seen a child engage in recently. Use the reflection questions to reconsider that behavior. Do you think anything new about the behavior? Would you change how you reacted, if given the chance?

Relationships and Physical Development

As you know, relationships are a crucial part of early childhood education (and of all education, really). Children are social creatures, and they learn in the context of social interactions.[7] Having close personal relationships with children allows teachers to know their abilities and needs, to communicate more effectively, to flexibly adjust plans to changing contexts. Relationships, in other words, improve teaching.

It's easy to see the importance of relationships in cognitive development and academic learning. When you know a child well, it's easier to tell when he needs a little hint on that math activity versus when he can keep puzzling it through himself. It's easier to change your writing lesson to meet the needs of a child who's having a bad day. It's easier to ask a child to keep working at a challenging project for just a little longer. It's easier to share a quiet moment reading a book.

Building resilience is more about physical and emotional development than cognitive, but relationships are equally important in every domain. In the context of responding to risky behaviors, having a positive relationship with the child makes all Four Steps easier and more effective. *Trusting* the child is easier when you know her capabilities. *Observing* the child is more effective when you know just what you're looking for. *Evaluating* the child's behavior is more effective when you have a deep understanding of the child and the context of her behavior. And when you're ready to *act*, your intervention will be more effective when the child has a positive relationship with you.

---

7   In the previous chapter we touched on Piaget's constructivist and sensorimotor frame for children's learning, and I mentioned that different models of learning are useful in different contexts. The idea here—that learning happens in the context of social interactions—is often credited to Lev Vygotsky, and is a cornerstone of the social-constructivist approach to learning and development. The two frames are in some senses mutually exclusive: Piaget says that all learning is an internal process of trial-and-error and problem solving; Vygotsky says that all learning is an external, socially-mediated process. Both can't be true, right? Actually, both perspectives on the learning process are valid, and both are useful for teachers and caregivers who want to support children's learning. When thinking about how to plan for hands-on learning and sensory play, I am inspired by Piaget's constructivism; when I think about my interactions with children playing, I am inspired by Vygotsky's social-constructivism.

Moreover, children will be more competent at risk taking when they feel they are surrounded by people who value and believe in them, because they will feel more sure of themselves and safe in their environment. Relationship-driven confidence is not the cockiness that leads to foolish risk taking; on the contrary, confidence that comes from relationships gives children the positive context in which to carefully consider their choices.

Want to build relationships with children around their physical development? It's not hard. All you have to do is engage in their physical activities. Going outside isn't recess, during which adults can check out, and the gym isn't a place to "get the wiggles out." Physical play is learning, and learning is better when teachers participate. If you participate in outdoor play as actively as you do in centers time, children will respond.

The analogy I like to use is that of emergent curriculum. When people first hear about emergent curriculum, they often say, "The curriculum follows the children's interests? So the kids just do whatever they want, and the teachers don't have to do anything?" But experienced educators know emergent curriculum isn't like that at all. In fact, emergent curriculum takes just as much planning, observation, supervision, and interaction as traditional curriculum models, if not more. The same is true of active physical play and the learning you want children to get from risk taking: it requires *more* interaction from teachers. The best growth always happens when children and caregivers are allies in learning, whether you're talking about academic learning or building resilience.

A teacher holds up a mat for children to crash into and try to push over.

Ways to Engage with Physical Play

- **Narrate.** Show your attention and approval by simply describing what you see. "You are climbing so high!" "Wow, you've been running a lot!" "Looks like you can't decide how to get down from there." "You're dizzy from all that spinning!" Some teachers enjoy the style of narration called *sportscasting*, in which you act as though you're describing what you're seeing to an audience: "She's climbing up the slide. Will she make it to the top? She looks confident. She's reaching for the bar and . . . she's at the top! The crowd goes wild!"

- **Encourage.** Offer a little boost of confidence. "You can do it!" "Look at you go!" "I know you can figure this out." "You did it!" Note that encouragement is not the same as praise. Praise is placing explicit value statements on children's activities—"Good job!"—and that kind of extrinsic motivation can backfire. Encouragement is simply voicing your confidence in the child's capabilities, and it's an effective way to support and connect with children.

- **Ask questions.** Show your interest by finding out more. "What are you working on?" "How will you solve that problem?" "What do you think will happen next?" Remember, open-ended questions like these, without clear right answers, are much more useful than closed ones (questions with a limited range of possible answers, such as "Are you having fun?" "Do you want to try the slide?").

- **Offer ideas.** Help children deepen their play by giving gentle hints. "I think you could reach if you put your foot *there*." "What if you put the bigger block on the bottom?" "You both say you want to be Spider-Man. It looks like there are *two* Spider-Mans!" Ideas work best when they extend what the children are already doing. Offering input isn't about your ideas; it's about helping the children find success with their ideas.

- **Play.** What better way to show you care than to join in the fun? Run. Climb. Jump. Be the bad guy. Help build the castle. Grab a shovel and start digging. You are a play expert—the children can learn so much from having you in the game. Be careful, though: it's easy for an adult to inadvertently become the star of the game. It's the children's learning we're after, so make sure to keep the focus on the children and their ideas, not on you and yours.

All of these approaches will help you build positive relationships with children in the context of their physical activity and development. Show children that you approve of and encourage their physical learning, that you take joy in their physical play. When the adults who care about children take joy in their physicality, children will take joy in it too.

Children and families at our schools built relationships during a roughhousing workshop. Activities like the pillow fight helped children feel powerful and connected to the adults who care for them.

The Self Skills

In using these approaches to children's physical play and risky behaviors, we support children in building what I call the *self skills*—a group of social and emotional capacities that are crucial in life and make up the lion's share of resilience. I'll describe each skill and how it connects to resilience, and then I'll detail specific strategies teachers can use to support each skill.

Self-Knowledge

Self-knowledge is the awareness of your own qualities, abilities, interests, and feelings. In the context of physical development, it's things like knowing whether you can make that jump, and whether you'll be upset if you fall and get hurt, and whether it'll be worth it to try anyway. Lots of our work in the classroom is about this skill, which is at the core of emotional development: the ability to understand oneself is a prerequisite for the ability to control oneself.

Self-Regulation

Also known more colloquially as *self-control*, self-regulation is the ability to exert some degree of choice over your feelings and behaviors. In a physical context, this means making good choices about what you do with your body—taking reasonable physical risks, for instance, or choosing to stop a game before someone gets hurt. In an emotional context, it means being able to make choices that will help you deal with big feelings—calming down when you're angry, for instance, or staying in control when you're excited. Although the physical and emotional sides of self-regulation look different from the outside, they're part of the same skill set and they grow together. Both are, essentially, the application of self-knowledge to choice making—you have to know an object is too heavy for you if you're going to make a good choice about throwing it; you have to know you're feeling scared if you're going to quell your fears.

Self-Confidence

Self-confidence is the belief in your own positive qualities and abilities. In a physical context it means being willing to try new things, try difficult things, take a risk or two. Self-confidence is different from *over*-confidence; healthy self-confidence rests on deep and accurate self-knowledge of your abilities and your limitations. Building self-confidence requires the positive feelings that come from succeeding in your choices—in other words, self-regulation. It's obvious that if you try to climb the jungle gym and make it to the top, you'll probably feel confident climbing it next time. But children also build self-confidence by having positive experiences choosing *not* to do something: when you decide that a jump is too high and find another way down, you learn that you're competent at taking care of yourself.

Self-Help

Self-help is the ability to do things for yourself. In a physical context, that means everything from climbing to the top of the climber and getting back down all by yourself to picking yourself up when you fall down. Self-help is a relative skill—you wouldn't call the same skills "self-help" in a two-year-old as a five-year-old. But at any age, self-help rests on healthy self-confidence—the belief that you *can* help yourself. For example, when you're climbing and your foot gets stuck, you have to believe that you *can* get it out if you're going to stay calm and figure it out. If you can't reach the monkey bars, you have to believe in your problem-solving ability if you're going to realize you can go get a stool to stand on. If you get a bump on the elbow, you have to believe in your ability to recover if you're going to go get yourself an ice pack.

Self-Comfort

Self-comfort is the ability to feel better when you're hurt or upset—essentially, self-help in upsetting circumstances. This can take practical forms, like getting yourself a Band-Aid when you scrape your knee or deciding to sit and take a break after a tumble. It can also take a less concrete shape: calming yourself when you're angry, for example. In some ways, it's a lot to ask of a young child—to access his self-knowledge, apply his self-regulation skills, feel confident, and help himself precisely when he's feeling most upset and vulnerable. But all together, it's these skills that make up resilience, and our approach to children's physical play helps them gradually develop these skills.

Building the Self Skills: Strategies and Techniques

Much of our practice as early childhood educators already centers on supporting children's social and emotional development. But there are some techniques that can specifically help build the self skills in the context of physical play.

Self-Knowledge

- **Narrate.** Building self-knowledge is a gradual process of learning from experiences. Teachers can help by giving voice to children's experiences so they can gain perspective. An easy way to do this is to simply describe a child's actions out loud: "You're climbing up that slide!" "You're running very fast!" Even more powerful, give voice to a child's emotional experiences: "You did not like that fall!" "You're up so high it's making you a little nervous." "Wow, you sure felt good when you made that jump!" Hearing their experiences reflected in words helps children to process them.

Self-Regulation

- **Call attention to self-knowledge.** If self-regulation is the application of self-knowledge, teachers can support children in this skill by helping them access what they know about themselves. This can take the form of asking strategic questions: "How are you feeling to be up so high?" or "How will you feel if you fall?"[8] You can also simply muse aloud in the child's hearing: "I remember last time you jumped from there, you felt so proud when you landed safely."

- **Support choice making.** Children learn to make good choices by making choices—good and bad—and learning from the consequences. That means we have to support children in making their own choices, even when we don't agree with those choices. Don't push children too hard to try a physical feat they're feeling nervous about: you might get a child to take a high jump she was scared of, and she might even enjoy it, but she'll

---

8   Remember, though, that these should not be rhetorical questions. The child's own lived experience is paramount. If you think a child is feeling scared to be up so high you might ask, "How are you feeling up there?," hoping that she will decide to climb down. But she might say, "I'm feeling good!" Don't contradict those feelings! You're trying to build self-regulation, which means you have to value mistakes as learning opportunities. If you feel the need to comment further, use an approach that acknowledges your different perspectives: "Huh! You were making a face that looked scared to me, but you say you're feeling good. How interesting that it seems different to the two of us!"

also learn not to trust her own feelings. Similarly, try not to stop a child from doing something when he's feeling confident and bold: you might stop him from getting injured, but you'll also teach him that he doesn't have to pay attention to his own safety, because someone will stop him if he goes too far. Overall, we have to *tolerate wrong choices*. Wrong choices are a necessary step along the way to making better choices.

- **Provide appropriate challenges.** As discussed earlier in this chapter, most children are naturally pretty good at finding appropriate physical challenges. They know when something is too difficult or too scary, and they don't try it. Unless, of course, appropriate challenges are not available. If there are no appropriate challenges, children will try to construct the challenges they need with the limited tools available. Two-year-olds need to climb, so if the only climber available is designed for five-year-olds, they'll climb on that, even if it's too dangerous. Five-year-olds need the sensation of being high up in the air, so if the only climber available is designed for the safety of two-year-olds, they'll find ways to climb on the outside of it or over the top of it, even if doing so is dangerous. If the children in your program are making lots of unsafe choices, ask yourself if the physical environment is offering them the challenges they need. Until you have an appropriate space for all the ages you serve, you will be fighting a constant battle around behavior, discipline, and boundaries—and missing important opportunities to support children's self-regulation.

Self-Confidence

- **Build relationships.** Children's self-image comes, in large part, from learning what the people they care about think about them. If you show children that you are confident in them, they will become more confident in themselves. So when they climb someplace high up and shout "Look at me!" for the hundredth time, look at them—yes, again—and continue to show them that you feel great about their physical development: "Look at you go!" "You're feeling great to be up so high!" Offer encouragement—"You can do it!"—and affirmation—"You did it!"[9] Show pride in children's accomplishments: "Mr. Hoover, you'll never guess how high your daughter climbed today!" And play, play, play! Be a mirror that shows children the most successful, competent versions of themselves, and that's who they'll learn how to be.

Self-Help

- **Provide opportunities for self-help.** Like everything else children learn, self-help skills are acquired in large part through practice. Therefore, your environment needs to provide children with opportunities to help themselves. Think about what children ask you for help with and see if you can find ways they could do it themselves. Do they ask for help climbing? Put some stools or milk crates in the yard that they can use to reach higher. Do they come to you when they need an ice pack? Consider having a child-accessible minifridge full of 'em. The more self-help options are available, the more children will help themselves.

- **Offer *optional* help.** Young children often need help, but caregivers sometimes provide more help than children want. In general, you should make yourself available to help children, but you shouldn't force help on a child who'd rather do it herself. You do this already for cognitive development—when a child is struggling with a puzzle, you don't just step in and put the pieces where they go. Instead, you sit nearby and ask if she wants help; you give quiet encouragement, but you let her puzzle it out. Similarly, when you see a child struggling to climb down from a high place, don't lift her down—stand nearby and say, "Let me know if you need a hand." Give her a chance to help herself.

- **Offer a *little* help.** When a child *does* ask for help, what kind of help should you give? Again, as with cognitive development, offer just enough support for the child to be successful, and no more. When the child working on a puzzle asks for help, you don't put all the pieces in place; you say,

---

9   Again, encouragement ("You can do it!") is different from praise ("Good job!"). Praise is about the value *you* place on the behavior; encouragement is about the value *the child* places on the behavior.

"Try turning that one around" or "I'll do the first one, you do the next one." Similarly, when the child trying to climb down asks for help, don't lift him down. Give a little hint, like "Where do you think you could put your hand?" or "Try putting your foot here." Or, if he really needs some help, guide his hands and feet to the right spots, but make sure *he's* the one doing the climbing. That way, when he gets to the bottom, you can honestly say, "You did it!" You want to make sure children feel safe and confident, but you don't want to remove challenge from their lives. Offer just enough help to ensure success.

Self-Comfort

- **Respond to children's need for comfort.** When children get hurt (or angry or frustrated), they usually reach out for comfort and support. You are a caregiver, first and foremost, and of course you must respond and meet children's needs. But while meeting the child's immediate need—to be comforted right now—keep in mind the child's long-term need: to build resilience and to gradually develop the ability to comfort herself. This is a tricky balance to strike. The next section describes a procedure for responding to injuries that helps to meet both kinds of need.

You'll notice that many of the strategies for building the self skills sound a lot like strategies for engaging with children's physical play. Isn't that convenient? It turns out that best practices accomplish multiple goals simultaneously. You can build relationships *and* support social and emotional skills *and* accomplish learning goals, all at the same time.

Responding to Injuries

As we've discussed, children *will* get injured sometimes. The question is, how can you make injury a learning experience?

All right, you've caught me. It's a trick question. Injury is always a learning experience. Indeed, all of children's experiences are learning experiences. But there are a lot of things children might learn from the experience of injury that you definitely don't want them to learn. You don't want them to learn "I can't do it." You don't want them to learn "Trying is scary." You don't want them to learn "I'm not safe." Those easy-to-learn lessons are damaging, and they undermine resilience.

The right question, of course, is how can you make injury a *positive* learning experience? Injury, by its very nature, is a perfect chance to learn all the self skills. It gives a child quite a bit of self-knowledge, and it's an opportunity to build self-regulation, self-confidence, self-help, and self-comfort. Some of that learning depends on the child, of course, but there's a lot teachers can do to support positive learning when an injury occurs.

Responding to injury is a lot like responding to risky behaviors, in that our natural caregiving response is very strong and immediate. So just as with risky behaviors, it helps to follow a four-part process to make sure you're meeting children's needs—both their need for comfort and their need for resilience.

1. Wait

Have you ever seen a child run, take a spill, get back up, and keep right on running? It happens all the time. Often children don't need any help, even for what looks (to us) like a big injury. If you step in when they don't need it, they'll learn from your behavior that little spills are a big deal that need lots of attention, and they'll expect that attention the next time. Take a breath, watch carefully, and see if the child actually needs you. Give her a chance to recover without your help.[10]

2. Wait Again

Okay, you've waited, and you've determined that the child does need help— she's crying and holding the injured body part. But if you swoop in and lift her off the ground, the lesson you teach is, "When I'm hurt, I don't need to

---

10 Of course, this step and the other three aren't relevant when you witness an injury that is obviously serious. When you see a big bash to the head or a fall from very high up you're going to swoop in to help immediately, and that is absolutely the right thing to do. But the vast majority of injuries at preschool are minor bumps and scrapes, many of which don't even leave a mark or require first aid. Use these steps to guide you in addressing the small, everyday injuries that are most common.

do anything at all—someone will take care of everything if I just cry loud enough." I've seen children with "learned helplessness" so severe that even a tiny bump makes them dissolve into an immobile puddle on the ground. We're trying to build self-confidence and self-help. We want children to learn that even when they're hurt, even when they need help, they can always take action to care for themselves. So squat down where you are, open your arms wide, put on your most sympathetic face, and say, "That looked like it hurt! Come here and get a hug!" Wait for them to come to you, so that they can build that very first of self-help skills: taking action.

3. Communicate

The way you communicate with a child in response to an injury has a huge effect on what the child learns from the experience. As with all communication, it's very important to listen to the child in this moment. Ask what happened, even if you saw the whole thing. The point is to help the child build self-knowledge and self-regulation, so you want to support the child in communicating about what happened. To that end, the child's perception of what happened is more important than the facts of the incident, in terms of what she learns from it. If the child is too upset to tell you what happened, of course, the first step is to help her calm down. Simply saying, "I'm right here, and I'll stay with you as long as you need until you're ready to talk about it" often makes a big difference.[11]

When it's your turn to talk, you have a tricky balancing act to pull off. On the one hand, you want the child to clearly understand that she is safe, that she doesn't have to worry, that you will protect her. On the other hand, you want the child to understand clearly that she is capable and powerful, and that you completely believe in her. There are a lot of common phrases that go too far in the first direction ("Oh, you poor baby!") or in the second ("Shake it

---

11 When working with preverbal children or children who are English-language learners, you will have to adapt this part of the process according to their abilities. The same strategies that work in other arenas to support language development are applicable here: listen attentively and patiently, gently encourage the children to say as much as they can, expand and extend children's short sentences, respond verbally to children's nonverbal communication, and so on.

off!").[12] Pay attention to which parts of your message the child is responding to and adjust accordingly. I usually start with something like, "That must have been quite a scare. I'm glad you're going to be okay."

4. Empower

Balance the child's need for comfort with his need for resilience by putting the child in control of the recovery process. Don't tell the child how to feel better—"Come take a break until you're ready" or "Let's get you an ice pack"—*ask him.* "What's going to help you feel better?" It's an incredibly powerful question. It builds self-confidence, because it shows you believe in his ability to self-regulate. It gives practice with self-help and self-comfort, and it builds self-knowledge. "What's going to help you feel better" puts the child in the driver's seat of his own recovery. (Though if you ask too early in the process, the child may not be done feeling upset, and the question will just make him feel out to sea: "I don't know what will make me feel better!" Choose your moment carefully.)

Sometimes a child won't know what will help him feel better, so you might give choices: "Do you want to go get a Band-Aid, or would you rather just sit and rest for a few minutes?" Sometimes, if a crowd of children has gathered, you might ask other children for input: "Has anyone else ever gotten a bump like Leo did? What makes *you* feel better when you get a bump like this?" And sometimes when you get to this point in the process, you'll find that the child already feels better, and that checking in was enough. In these moments you might say, "Do you need to do something to feel better, or would you rather go back and keep playing?" When the child is empowered in his own recovery, the recovery is faster and more effective.

<div align="center">~~~~~~~~~~~~~~~~~~~</div>

---

12 Of course, those approaches tend to be applied in a gendered way. Boys are more often encouraged to be tough, and girls are more often coddled—a disparity that is harmful to both.

This approach isn't a set of hard-and-fast rules, of course. Every child and every injury is different, and you'll adjust according to the needs of the situation. But practicing this process as a frame for responding to injury can help you focus on the productive learning experience that injury can be and help you best meet children's needs in that stressful moment.

Building a Culture of Resilience

This chapter has described a variety of tools and practices to help children build resilience in the context of physical play—ways to encourage positive and balanced risk taking, ways to reduce harm from risk taking, ways to build children's social and emotional skills around physical play, ways to build relationships around physical play. Each of these practices could stand alone as a strategy to promote resilience. But taken together, they help create a culture of resilience in your program.

Teacher versus children tug-o-war is a great way to build confidence and teamwork—and most adults are a match for a dozen three-year-olds.

A culture is a set of shared values, expectations, and practices within a community. The approaches in this chapter help develop those things among the children you teach. The children will begin to place value on physical play and physical challenge; they will expect to learn and develop in physical ways at school; and they'll engage in shared practices like self-care and choice making. They will share a school culture of resilience.

Culture is inertial: it's hard to make changes in it. When you decide you want to incorporate resilience into your program's culture, it's going to take time, effort, and patience to make a change before you start seeing results. But by the same token, once a culture is in place, it becomes the norm. When resilience is woven into your school's culture, it is equally woven into the children's lives and identities. Resilience isn't something they have to learn—it's something they *do*. The school's practices will make the children more resilient.

Chapter Postscript: Working with Children with Disabilities

Children with disabilities are often prevented from taking risks. Any kind of disability—physical, cognitive, emotional—tends to bring out adults' impulse to protect. Even adults who happily let typically developing children leap off the climber can balk when a child with a disability tries the same stunt. We may think, "She's not ready for that." Or, "He's got enough to deal with. Why risk adding an injury to that?" Or, "What if something happens?" But the fact is, it's just as important to let children with disabilities experience the benefits of risk taking as it is for typically developing children. Resilience is a skill *all* children need.

The phrase *dignity of risk* was coined in the early 1970s in the context of caring for adults with cognitive disabilities; it has since been used in the context of caring for both adults and children with all types of disabilities, as well as care of the elderly. The idea is that people with disabilities must be afforded the same respect we afford everyone else, which includes the right to make choices we disagree with. Self-determination is an important part of human development, and the right to learn from trial and error, from successes and failures, is a part of that.

Of course, you should coordinate with a child's family in addressing the specific needs associated with a child's disability. A child with a traumatic brain injury probably shouldn't leap from high places; a child who uses a wheelchair probably won't be able to leap at all. In cases such as these, think about modified versions of activities: Can the child accomplish a lower jump? Do a different kind of crash? Climb up high without jumping? The child's therapists and service providers can offer suggestions for modified activities when that's appropriate. Remember, if a child needs extra support in order to participate, that support should be part of the child's IEP. But many disabilities don't call for any extra support or need for modified risk—children with autism or Down syndrome are entirely capable of leaping off the climber along with the other children.

Resilience is an especially relevant concept when working with children with disabilities. Almost by definition, disabilities make interactions with the world more trying, more full of challenges, frustrations, and setbacks—just the things resilience skills address. Autism, for instance, is a condition that makes sensory and social input more overwhelming; learning to cope gracefully with these overwhelming inputs is an important developmental task for children with autism spectrum disorder.

It's crucial to remember, however, that *the disability is not the child*. It's easy to get caught up in meeting the special needs associated with a child's disabilities and forget that the child has all the other needs typically developing children do as well. A child with spina bifida may need support with movement and a degree of physical protection, but she also needs adventure and exploration and challenge and risk, just like every other child.

While many children with disabilities have a particular need for resilience, the very same children often develop unusually strong resilience. A lifetime of negotiating an environment that is not well set up to meet your needs—your physical, sensory, social, and cognitive needs—naturally pushes you to build the skills to bounce back from frustrations, disappointments, and challenges. Children who grow up with disabilities are often used to needing to enter new situations with creativity, flexibility, and courage. Along with presuming that children with disabilities are competent to make their own choices, we can presume that they enter our programs with resilience as well.

Overall, the principles of building resilience discussed in this chapter and in this book apply just as much to children with disabilities as to typically developing children. In particular, consider the following approaches:

- Create an environment with appropriate and graduated challenges.[13]

- Help children calibrate the right level of risk taking for themselves.

---

13 The principles of inclusive design are tools to create environments that meet a wide range of needs for a wide range of children. Familiarizing yourself with these principles will help you create a physical space that will increase access to play opportunities for all children, not just children with disabilities. Resources on inclusive design can be found in the "Physical Environment (Gross Motor)" section of appendix B.

- Trust children to make decisions about risk and value "mistakes" as learning experiences.

- Carefully reflect on how you respond to children's risky behaviors.

- Build relationships in the context of physical play.

- Provide opportunities for self-help.

- When you help children, make sure they have the option to turn down your help.

- Offer children just enough help to allow them to be successful, no more.

- Empower children through your response to injuries.

Go back through this chapter and read the sections on the approaches in the preceding list, keeping in mind the diverse needs of children with disabilities. For more resources, see appendix B.

~ 4 ~

Working with Families

If our goal is to help children build resilience, our approach must include their families.

The inclusion of families is an important aspect of achieving *any* educational goals, of course. Best practice is for families to be involved as fully as possible in your program, for so many reasons. Whatever you are teaching children—from basic arithmetic to conflict-resolution skills—you'll teach it better if families are teaching it at home too. More important, if there are communication and agreement between families and schools about your vision and values for children, everyone's work will support and reinforce each other's. Not to mention the fact that children are inextricable parts of their families, so the better you meet families' needs, the better you'll be meeting children's needs.

When we work to build children's resilience in the context of active physical play, it is both particularly necessary and (sometimes) particularly challenging to see eye to eye with families. While both families and teachers have children's best interests as their primary goal, it is sometimes difficult to see issues of physicality in the same way. A teacher who has seen a child for the whole day can easily look at a child's scraped knee and see the amazing play experience that caused it, or look at a bump on a child's forehead and see the important learning experience that came with it. But a parent or family member walking into the room at pickup time doesn't see that context; they see only the visible injury. Even when a family believes in the importance of physical play and resilience, injuries simply feel different when it's *your kid* getting hurt.

Safety is an extremely important issue to families, and rightly so. We know children can't learn if they don't feel safe; in just the same way, families can't engage with your school if they don't feel their children are safe. The word *feel* is important—just because we feel children are safe enough doesn't mean their families will feel the same way. It's vital for us not only to ensure children's safety but also to communicate to families how we ensure their children's safety.

Another way to say all this is that just as we have responsibilities to children, we also have responsibilities to their families. Our primary responsibility to families is to provide their children with the best care and learning we're capable of, but our responsibilities go further. The National Association for the Education of Young Children's (NAEYC) *Code of Ethical Conduct and Statement of Commitment* puts it this way: "Families are of primary importance in children's development. Because the family and the early childhood practitioner have a common interest in the child's well-being, we acknowledge a primary responsibility to bring about communication, cooperation, and collaboration between the home and early childhood program in ways that enhance the child's development" (National Association for the Education of Young Children 2005). In other words, our relationships with the families we serve connect directly to how we teach and care for their children.

As we set goals for our work with children around resilience, we must also set goals for our work with their families. The first goal is to *build trusting relationships with families in the context of children's physical development and resilience*. Families need to feel confident in the care we give their children.

Beyond that, families need to feel their needs and values are heard, understood, and respected—in particular (for our purposes here) their needs and values regarding learning, play, physical and emotional development, and health and safety. And we, as educators, have needs and values concerning these topics that we must communicate to families. Thus, our second goal is to *build shared understanding and values around children's resilience, joy, and learning*. By working toward these goals, we can be most effective in helping children in becoming resilient.

REFLECTION

Think of the families in your program. What needs do they have around their children's safety? What are their values regarding physical and emotional development? What do they think about their children's play?

If you don't know the answers to these questions, how could you find out? If you feel you do know the answers to these questions, how do you know? How sure are you? Are you thinking of all the families you serve, or just some of them?

Communication

Let's talk about building trust with families. There are a lot of things on which we need families to trust us. We need them to trust that their children are well cared for and safe; that we have their child's best interests at heart; that we know what we're doing in terms of early childhood theory and practice. You could tell them all of these things—"Dear families, We know what we're doing and your kids are safe!"—but of course, that's not how trust works. Trust is made of a complicated mix of perception and experience and emotion. You've worked hard on your practice with children, and that makes you trustworthy—but being trustworthy isn't the same as being trusted.

Irene Carney, executive director of Sabot at Stony Point in Richmond, Virginia (more on that school in chapter 5), points out that "young families are in an anxious stage of their lives"—many of them are caring for young children for the first time and are especially attuned to all the dangers in the world. She says that in building trust around health and safety, what feels like overcommunication to teachers can be the amount of communication that many young families need. Phone calls about minor injuries and rigorous documentation of small events can assure families that their children are being well cared for. She also says that visible demonstrations of responsible practices are helpful. In an unusual and dramatic incident several years ago, their school needed to go into lockdown for several hours. Afterward, far from being concerned, many parents commented, "Wow, you really have clear procedures for ensuring safety!" While it wasn't the school's intention, the lockdown served to show how seriously the school took safety.

These examples are not tricks to gain trust; trust can't be manufactured or faked or forced. You give your trust, in general, to people who demonstrate trustworthiness over time. You give your trust to people whom you know well, and who know you well. You give your trust to people who understand and respect you, and whom you understand and respect. In short, trust emerges from positive relationships.

Building positive relationships isn't easy or simple, of course. There are entire books about building positive relationships between schools and families (for recommendations, see appendix B). Relationships take work, time, attention, and energy. Most of all, they take communication. Communication is the special sauce that will build your interactions into relationships, created from mutual understanding and respect, leading to trust.

It bears mentioning, at this point, that trust, relationships, and communication are all intrinsically two-way streets. Trust isn't just an issue of families trusting you; you need to trust them as well, by believing in their good intentions, their values, their knowledge of their children. Relationships aren't just there for families to feel good; you need to commit to relationships with families as well. And communication isn't just about your being good at explaining what your school is doing—receptive communication, as you know from your work with children, is just as important as expressive communication. We'll refer to the talking and listening parts of communication separately at times, but of course they rely on each other to be effective.

Talking isn't just words coming out of your mouth—it's everything you do to express yourself and what your school is doing. Your talking might include e-mails to families, documentation on your school walls, written materials on your website, or the talking points you hit during your open houses—all in addition to face-to-face, one-on-one conversations. All the ways you and your school show families who you are—what you value, what your goals are, what your process looks like—are ways of talking. To build trusting relationships with families, simply expressing ideas is not enough. We must express ourselves honestly and clearly, so that families know exactly who we are and what we do. We need to be transparent about our practices and beliefs and give as complete a picture of who we are as possible, so that families can trust what we do.

Listening is not just hearing what others tell you in face-to-face conversations; it's everything you do to understand their points of view. It includes asking questions and soliciting input; creating opportunities for sharing thoughts and a culture of responsiveness to input; holding conversations with groups of families as well as individual family members; attending not only to what is said but also to what isn't. To build trusting relationships with families, you have to work to understand their points of view completely. Just asking what they think isn't enough—you have to go out of your way to know their values, their contexts, their cultures. You have to actively solicit input and genuinely value dissent. You have to build a dialogue and be willing to be changed by that conversation. We need to show that we value and respect the families we work with.

Genuine communication with families is always good practice for educators. In the coming sections, I'll lay out some specific strategies for effective communication in the context of building resilience in young children.

Effective Talking: Advertising and Selling

When we want to convey an idea to a group of young children, we know we need to express it multiple times in multiple ways. For instance, if we want to explain to children how to use scissors safely, we might put on a puppet show about scissor safety at circle time, then have a small-group, hands-on activity with scissors at centers time, then have a conversation about scissor safety at the lunch table . . . and then do it all again the next day. The same principle applies to expressing an idea to adults. To communicate effectively with a group of families, you need to present an idea at different times in different ways, so that different families can access the idea in the way that makes the most sense for them. This is not to say that families are stupid or hard to communicate with, any more than children are stupid or hard to communicate with. But we recognize that, like children, each adult is a unique individual; for groups of individuals to understand us, we need a range of strategies and opportunities for communicating with them.

In this case, the idea we're communicating is about resilience, and what your school does to promote it. You believe children's physical and emotional development are important. You value resilience and know that your teaching practices have a role in building resilience in children. You make careful, thoughtful decisions about how you will interact with children's physical play and risk taking and their injuries and recoveries. These beliefs and practices are part of who you are as an educator and as a program. You need to advertise and sell those values and practices.

Advertise and *sell* are words that have picked up the tarnish of crass commercialism, but they're important aspects of communication. *Advertising* means clearly expressing who you are and what you do. *Selling* means convincing people that who you are and what you do are good. In other words, if you believe in your teaching practice, advertising and selling are simply parts of effective talking.

Advertising: Expressing Your Values and Practices Clearly

In general, you want people to know all the great things about your program. People seek your program out when they know about your amazing curriculum, your vigorous community, your caring and committed staff. Other aspects of your program might attract certain families while deterring families who might not be a good match for you. For instance, if your program puts particular emphasis on early academics, families who value academics will seek you out, and families who place more value on social and emotional learning may rightly look somewhere else. Everyone—caregivers, families, children—is best served when there is a good match between the family's and the program's values.

You want families to clearly know your stance on resilience and how it figures into your programming. If your approach to risk taking, injury, and physicality is part of your philosophy of education (as I hope, by this point, it is), families should know about it and have an opportunity to opt in or out of your program. Topics such as injury are sensitive, so families need to know from the get-go what they're signing up for. Some families will learn about this part of your program and say, "This isn't for us"—but just as many will actively seek you out because of it.[1]

Advertising your approach to resilience can and should be part of all the ways you already tell families who you are:

- Do you have a flyer you distribute with photos of children reading books and working on math? Add a photo of a child jumping from a high place, with a caption like, "When children take appropriate physical risks, they build self-confidence and resilience!"

---

1   Of course, like any advertising, it's not just a question of saying what you do—how you say it is very important. If McDonald's proclaimed, "We use the cheapest possible ingredients to give you passable but very cheap food," no one would eat there, even though it's true; instead, they advertise their "Extra Value Meals," which sound much more attractive, despite meaning essentially the same thing. Similarly, if your program's materials said, "We give children the opportunity to get hurt in hopes that they'll toughen up," that wouldn't be a very attractive message to prospective families. How you say it matters. "One of the ways we support children in becoming resilient is to support them in making choices about their physical play, learning how to care for themselves and to recover from injuries." The second version has the same literal meaning as the first, but the wording provides a very different message.

- Do you have a website that describes your approach to children's learning and development? Add a section on the importance of building resilience and some of the ways your program supports that learning.

- Do you have a public Facebook page or Twitter feed where you share glimpses into learning at your program? Make resilience a topic you explore there, with photos of children engaged in active play or descriptions of how you support children with injuries.

- Do you give tours to prospective families, where you show off the various materials your program uses to support learning? Spend some time talking about the jungle gym or the climbing tree. Do you let prospective families observe a normal day in progress? Let them watch physical play and describe the important ways caregivers support the children in your program.

Recently I had an opportunity to visit the Miquon School, an independent school (pre-K through sixth grade) in a wooded area north of Philadelphia. Children at Miquon spend a significant portion of every day playing in the trees, on the hills, in the creek—sometimes without direct adult supervision. Visitors to the school see children chasing through the woods, swinging sticks, having snowball fights. The first thing I thought when I visited was, "Wow, this place sure knows how to advertise its approach to resilience!"

Outdoor play area for young children at the Miquon School.

Young children at Miquon School play without direct adult supervision.

No one could walk through their campus and not ask, "What do you do when kids get hurt? Why aren't there more adults watching? How do you make sure children are safe?" Such questions are, of course, exactly what they want people to ask, because they have well-developed answers to them that they are eager to share. Whether or not you agree with Miquon's approach to building resilience, you can't help knowing what their approach is. Families who choose to send their children to Miquon know what they're getting.

Your school may not have a physical layout that displays resilience-related qualities so obviously—how many of us are lucky enough to have a campus in the woods? So you need to find other ways to be just as clear about your program. You need to advertise.[2]

Selling: Convincing People Your Values and Practices Are Good

When people know who your school is and how you approach resilience, they have a chance to opt in or out of your school, and that's great—but if you stop

---

2   Of course, this principle is true not just of your approach to resilience but your approach to your entire program as well. People should know exactly who you are and why you do what you do. See appendix B for resources on communicating clearly about your school.

there, you miss an important opportunity. Don't just tell people what you do—convince them that what you do is great.

More specifically, when the topic of resilience comes up with prospective families[3]—and you will make sure it does, as discussed earlier—don't just say that you build resilience. Take the opportunity to talk about the connections between resilience and academic learning (see "Risk and Early Childhood" in chapter 2). Bring up the research on the importance of resilience to long-term success in school and in life (see "Physical Development and Beyond" in appendix B). Bring up your personal experiences helping children recover from injury and upset.

A conversation about resilience—which, again, you will be creating every opportunity for—is a chance to sell people on your approach. Don't be shy about showing how great you are!

···················

The way you teach is valuable and important. Your education and experience combine to give you expertise, which informs your values and your practices. The ways in which you support children's resilience are worth telling people about and convincing people of. Advertising and selling your practices aren't crass commercialism—they're good pedagogy. You're not just a teacher of children; you're also a teacher of families. So share your expertise with them, and let them learn from your example!

For more resources and strategies for communicating with families, see appendix B.

Effective Listening: Building Dialogue

> **REFLECTION**
>
> Think about the ways your program already advertises and sells. What approaches do you already use to let prospective and current families know who you are, what you value, how you teach? Are there any new techniques that would be easy to incorporate? Is resilience a topic you include in these approaches? If not, how could you incorporate it?

No matter how effective you are at expressing to families what you do, if your goal is to build trusting relationships, talking will never be enough. Trust is

---

3   Or when it comes up with current families, colleagues, community members, policy makers . . .

built through an exchange of information and ideas, a conversation, a dia-logue. For that to happen, you've got to be just as good at listening.

Actually, you've got to be better at listening than talking, because families may not come right out and say what they have to say. There are a lot of struc-tural barriers to families telling caregivers what's on their minds:

- **Inexperience**—Many families of young children are new to caring for children and may not know what their opinions are or may feel they have nothing valuable to contribute to a conversation yet.

- **Expertise**—Families often feel that the caregivers are the experts about what's best for children, so they choose not to speak up, even if they dis-agree with a program's practice.

- **Bad listening**—Many families have had experiences with caregivers or schools that ignore or argue with their opinions, so they figure it's not worth expressing opinions to "experts" who won't listen.

- **Authority**—Families may hold cultural values that discourage direct or open disagreement with authority figures, such as teachers and adminis-trators.

- **Personal history**—Families may have had negative experiences with programs and schools in the past, perhaps in their own childhoods, which have caused them to lose confidence in the possibilities of communicating with caregivers.

A caregiver may, with the best of intentions, try to listen to what families have to say, but unless she actively works to counteract these barriers, many families will not express all they have to say.

Norms of communication are often set very early in relationships, so it's important for *your first interactions with families* to actively express how much you value their perspectives. For instance, on tours for prospective families, before you start talking about your school's program, consider asking, "What are you looking for in a school? What are you hoping for in the next few years of your child's life?" As you begin to describe your school, you'll already have a basis on which to say, "Here's how our program connects with your values; here are ways we differ." The same questions are also great discussion points in start-of-year home visits, if you are lucky enough to work in a program that provides for them.

Similarly, at my school's Back to School Night each September, we ask families icebreaker questions such as, "When you think of your children in twenty years, what qualities will you want them to have?" or "What skills does an adult need in order to have a good life?" Then throughout the evening we take every opportunity to find links between our practices and families' values. The conversation can be extremely powerful, because we're all communicating from a place of understanding one another's values.

One-on-one conversations are often the best way to connect with others and hear their perspectives. But the structure of a preschool day can make spontaneous conversations difficult: the most convenient times—pickup and drop-off, when we're all in the same room—are often the least convenient situations—teachers are juggling a million things and families are trying to get out the door. It's important to actively create other opportunities for conversations, and not simply assume that families will make it happen if they have something to say. If a family member brings something up ("I'm wondering about his speech development" or "We're going to be moving to a new house" or "I'm concerned about the bump on the head she got yesterday"), make it a point to schedule a phone conversation or get coverage in your room so that you can give your full attention. Making a habit of this demonstrates to families that you care what they have to say.

The most formal conversation with a family is often the parent-teacher conference. Teachers have a lot to tell families at these meetings—but it's just as important to listen. I make a point of starting conferences by asking, "How are things going? How does your child's time at school seem to you? Is there anything on your mind that you want to make sure to talk about?" If I'm sharing information about, say, a challenging behavior I've seen at school, I always ask, "Does that match what you've seen at home? How does the behavior seem to you? Are there strategies you use for this at home that we can try at school?" Actively asking for a family's perspective and experiences with their child makes it clear the conversation is a two-way street.

There are also many opportunities you can create for asynchronous conversations—communication in which multiple parties participate at different times. Does your school have a Facebook page or a Twitter feed? Encourage families to post articles of interest to your wall. Does your school keep a blog?

Encourage families to comment on what they read. You don't need computers for this kind of communication either. I know a school where every visitor is handed a quick form to fill out before they leave, asking for responses such as "Something interesting I noticed at school was _____" and "Something I saw that I wondered about was _____." These forms are then posted on a bulletin board as a kind of public conversation.

Remember, not every family feels equally comfortable communicating in the same ways. For some, one-on-one, face-to-face conversations may work fine. But you should also make opportunities for staff to talk to families in groups (like a discussion night at school), and for families to communicate through writing (for example, with a classroom e-mail account), and for families to communicate anonymously (such as a classroom suggestion box). There will always be families who feel more comfortable with a different mode of communication. But by providing communication options, you're signaling to all families that you take their input seriously and that you're going out of your way to receive it. By setting that tone, you'll make families feel more comfortable telling you what's on their minds.

In the preceding section, we discussed how a principle of talking with children—expressing the same idea in multiple ways at multiple times—also applies to adults. The same is true of listening to children and their families. When we try to understand children's knowledge and thinking, we know we can't simply ask them what they know and be done with it. Authentic assessment requires giving children many opportunities to express their knowledge and thinking in many different ways. For instance, if we want to know about a child's knowledge of the alphabet, we might play with the magnet letters with her and see what she says, and then read a familiar book with her and ask her to point out letters she knows, and then later give her the opportunity to dictate a story and ask her to sign her name at the bottom, and so on. The same principle applies to listening to families and other adults: you need to give them many different opportunities to be heard in many different ways. Look at all the avenues for listening just described, and remember that the more of them you open up, the more fully you'll be able to hear what families have to say.

All of these approaches, and more, are ways you can build a culture of listening at your school, for ensuring that opportunities for families to share their perspectives are built into both the structure and the mind-set of your program. They will help you build communication around any aspect of your program, from your literacy curriculum to your approach to community building. These approaches are particularly important when communicating about physicality and resilience. As discussed at the beginning of this chapter, these are often emotionally charged issues for families, and it's easy for families to feel threatened or defensive—and therefore less communicative—when safety or injury is on the table. You can't, for example, start your very first conversation about values when someone's child is injured and expect each other to be on the same page. You need to have already laid a lot of communication groundwork.

In all the conversations you create with families concerning values, make sure to include issues of physicality, safety, risk, and resilience. When you ask families for their points of view, ask open-ended and family-specific questions:

- How do you feel about your child's physical development?

- What are your child's favorite physical games and activities?

- What kinds of physical risks and challenges does your child seek?

- How do you feel about the physical risks and challenges your child seeks?

- How do you think and talk about safety in your family?

- How does your child react to injuries?

- What helps your child recover from setbacks, injuries, or upsets?

These kinds of questions help you in more ways than one. They help you gain important information about families' perspectives on these issues. More broadly, they contribute to a school culture where families' perspectives are solicited and valued. And, in a quiet way, the existence of these questions demonstrates that issues of physicality, safety, risk, and resilience are important to you and your program. Simply bringing up the issues encourages families to examine their own values and ideas—and opens the door for productive conversations going forward.

"Going forward" is important. Building dialogue isn't a single-occasion, one-and-done activity. Dialogue is ongoing and needs to be nurtured over time. Families' perspectives will evolve as their children age, as they gain new experiences, as they are more exposed to your program. The conversation you'll have with a family at the start of year one is different from the conversation at the end of year two—so make sure to have them both. And, while you're at it, see if you can get the year one and year two families talking to one another as well. The more communication there is in every direction, the further you'll be in creating a culture of trusting relationships.

Disagreements: What to Do When You Don't See Eye to Eye

No matter how much high-quality talking you do, no matter how deep your listening, you will sometimes find yourself in a disagreement with one or more of the families in your program. In fact, sometimes your excellent communication will bring up more disagreements—when people feel comfortable sharing their points of view, those points of view will sometimes conflict. That's okay! The trusting relationships you're building will make it possible for you to navigate disagreements and emerge stronger on the other side. But there are some strategies that can help you use conflicts as an opportunity to build relationships and communication and to support your goal of building children's resilience.

As a lesson in what *not* to do, I'll relate a story a former colleague of mine told about a former workplace of hers. In the two-year-olds' room at this school, they had been doing a beading activity, and several children stuck beads up their noses. No one was seriously hurt, but it was scary, and families were understandably upset. A group of parents demanded that beads no longer be used with such young children. The director of the school responded with something like, "We think beads are an important activity for fine-motor development, and we won't be removing them. Our school does not let parents dictate policy." As you might imagine, many families were incensed by this response, and a few of them left the school.

Let's think about some things you could do to avoid the mistakes this director made and the outcomes this director caused:

- **Listen more than you talk.** In a conflict, people have a deep need to be understood, which means we all tend to lean more toward the talking side rather than the listening side of communication. "If I could just explain, they'd see how right I am!" we seem to think. But this tendency actually makes it more difficult to resolve a conflict. In the bead story, the upset families didn't need to have fine-motor development explained to them; they needed to ensure their children's safety. If you can suppress your urge to explain, even temporarily, you'll have a much easier time hearing families' needs, and families will know that you value what they have to say. This director could have entered the conversation saying, "I hear that you're upset about what happened. I want to make sure I fully understand your point of view before I respond; please tell me more about how you see the situation."

- **Look for common ground.** When you're not seeing eye to eye, it helps to work from the places where you do agree. In the preceding story, the director and the families couldn't recognize their shared goals and values when they were in the middle of the conflict. "These families don't seem to value fine-motor development!" the director seemed to think. And the families might have thought, "How can this director not value safety?" Things might have gone more smoothly if the director had said, "What we all value most is the well-being of your children. Let's problem solve about how to achieve that in a way that makes sense to everyone." This can be a useful time to look at the program's mission or at those foundational conversations in which you and the families discussed your goals for children. It would have been so valuable if this director could have started this conversation by saying, "We've all talked together several times about the value of resilience. Let's think about how we can use that value to approach this situation."

- **Disagree respectfully.** When the director in the story said, "Our school does not let parents dictate policy," she was essentially saying, "I don't care what you think." No wonder families were upset! It's okay to have different opinions, points of view, values—but it's not okay to be dismissive or disrespectful. Respectful disagreement is only possible when you've truly listened. This director could have held her ground on the policy, while still making families feel heard, if she had said something like, "I hear your concerns about safety, and I can understand why you're upset. But I think we have different views of this situation. I believe that the benefits of fine-motor development this activity provides are so great that it's important to keep the existing policy in place."

- **Be open to change.** When you truly listen to another's point of view, you may discover that your initial position was wrong. That's okay. In fact, it's better than okay—it's a fantastic opportunity! You have a chance to be a better teacher or a better school tomorrow than you were today. The director could have said, "After listening to your concerns, I realize we made an error. We were so focused on developing fine-motor skills that we lost sight of safety. Thank you for bringing this to our attention and being willing to communicate about it." This is not an easy thing to say, of course—it's quite a challenge to admit you were wrong, especially if you're an "expert" taking input from a "nonexpert." But honest communication is a powerful way to build trust. And it provides a model for families to be able to change their minds as well, leading to a culture where everyone can learn and grow.

> **REFLECTION**
>
> Have you ever had a conflict with a family (with regard to physicality and resilience, or something else)? What parts of your communication worked well in that instance? What parts would you do differently if it happened again?

What to Do When You Really Don't See Eye to Eye

Sadly, not every conflict can be resolved. If you reach a fundamental difference of values with a family, no amount of high-quality communication will help you reach common ground. Your program may believe, as an institution, that small bruises and scrapes are acceptable in the pursuit of resilience; a family may believe that no degree of injury is acceptable. In this case, a family may decide to leave your program—and that should be okay. If a program cannot meet a family's needs for any reason, including a fundamental difference of beliefs, then it's just not a good fit. Your advertising and selling practices will go a long way toward avoiding that outcome, but no approach ensures 100 percent compatibility between a school and its families. Despite your best efforts, a family could miss your messages about physicality and learning. Or they might have been attracted to the ideas but find that the reality makes them uncomfortable. Or they might have felt that the issue was something they could compromise on, and it turns out they just can't.

Even when a family has already decided to part ways with a program, good communication can still serve everyone's needs. Think about holding an exit interview with the departing family or providing them with an exit survey. Sometimes it's easier to communicate when the decision's already been made.

- **Listening.** It still behooves you to ask for the family's point of view, even on their way out the door. "We'd like our school to be able to avoid reaching this point with other families in the future. Your perspective can help us avoid mistakes in the future. I know we've discussed this already, but I want to make sure I fully understand. Would you mind telling me one more time what needs our school isn't meeting for your family? Are there things that we could do in the future to avoid this outcome?" It's not a time to argue or convince; the time for advertising and selling has passed. It's a time for you to learn from the experiences of those you're trying to serve. So ask good questions and listen carefully.

- **Talking.** You can better serve all families in your program by thoughtfully communicating with this one, even though they're leaving. See if you can describe the conflict in a way that honors both parties' perspectives. For instance, "It seems to me that when it comes right down to it, your family places a high value on avoiding injuries, and our program places a high value on building resilience." This family will assuredly talk with other families—families still enrolled, families in the neighborhood—about why and how they left your program. If you and this family can manage to have a shared, respectful understanding of the conflict, the family is more likely to be able to share that perspective with others—others who will, in turn, have a better understanding of your program's identity and values.

Talking to Families about Injuries

Children at your school are going to get hurt. When they do, you'll have to talk to their families about what happened. This can be a nerve-racking experience for teachers. It's easy to feel as though we failed in keeping the child safe or to think that the family will believe we failed in keeping the child safe. It's easy to get defensive or overapologetic or awkward.

But it doesn't have to feel like that. In chapter 3, we talked about injuries as opportunities to build children's resilience; they're also opportunities to work with families on issues of resilience. Conversations about injuries are perfect times to discuss physical development, self-regulation, and self-care skills. An injury shouldn't be the *only* time you talk about these issues, however, and it shouldn't be the *first* time—these conversations will go much better when they happen in the context of a continuing dialogue about resilience.

When you talk to a family member about their child getting injured,[4] here are some approaches that can help:

- **Tell a story.** An injury makes more sense, and therefore feels less upsetting, when it has a context. If all a parent hears is, "He got hit on the head," then the injury itself is all the parent will have to think about. If you include the context of the incident, and particularly what learning was happening, the family member will be much more able to see that the injury itself wasn't as important as what else was going on. "Hi, this is Jarrod calling from preschool. Terry is fine,[5] but I wanted to let you know he got quite a bonk on the head. He and his friends were building this amazing structure with the big blocks, working so hard together to build a bridge that they could walk across. Such great teamwork! But a block slipped and hit Terry. He's doing fine, but I wanted to let you know there's a raised bump on his head that you'll see when you pick him up today."

- **Talk about strengths.** Don't just talk about what went wrong; talk about what went right. "She was running and she slipped" makes it sound like

---

4   Every school should have clear policies about what injuries warrant a phone call or an accident report (more on accident reports in chapter 6) or other responses. Personally, I fill out a report for any injury that required more first aid than a single Band-Aid or a brief rest with an ice pack; any injury that comes with a story the child is likely to tell the family later; or any injury that is part of a pattern of injuries. I'll phone a family for any injury that leaves a significant mark or any injury to the face or head—I don't want any family member to come at pickup time and see something to worry about before I get a chance to relate what happened. I also make a point of phoning families who are especially worried about injuries.

5   I start every phone call during the school day with "So-and-so is fine." Most family members, when they see the school's number on caller ID, will have a momentary flash of "Oh my god—is my child in the hospital?" Best to dispel that right away.

maybe she shouldn't have been running; "She ran around the track fifteen times, but on the sixteenth time she slipped" makes it clear that the child was running competently. "He ran his bike into a tree" makes it sound like he's a klutz who shouldn't be allowed on a bike; "He ran his bike into a tree, but after that he was more careful to look where he was going" makes it clear that it was a learning opportunity. "She got hurt and had to take a break from playing for a while" makes it sound like the child was crying alone and left out; "She had to take a break, so a few friends came and sat with her until she felt better" makes it clear that she's a part of a caring community.

- **Talk about recovery.** When you're describing what happened, make sure "what happened" includes how the child felt better. Not just the first aid steps (though you should mention those too) but also the emotional-recovery steps. "He decided to sit out for a few minutes, but when I asked him two minutes later he said he was ready to play again." "It was enough of a bonk to leave a bruise, but she said she just wanted to keep playing." "His friend came over and gave him a hug, and he said that made him feel better." When you include the recovery in your narrative of what happened, it helps families see their children as capable and resilient.

Telling families about their children's injuries can be difficult, but such reports provide important opportunities to help families think in terms of resilience so that they can help their children build resilience.

> **REFLECTION**
>
> Think about times when you've told families about injuries. When has a family reacted better than you expected when hearing about their child's injury? When is a time a family has reacted worse than you hoped? What made the difference? What did the family that reacted poorly need that they weren't getting? How could you have helped them?

Family Education

We are not just teachers of children but also teachers of families. In teacher-family relationships, families are the experts on their own children, but we are the experts on children in general. Families look to us for our education and our experience to help them know what children need, and how to give it to them.

There is a lot that families can learn from us. We can teach them about our philosophies and values and perspectives on children's development and learning. We can teach them a set of skills they can use to support and teach their children. We can teach them that safety doesn't begin and end with avoiding injury. We can teach them that risk is valuable in children's lives. We can teach them to encourage adventurous physical play. We can teach them to support their children's resilience.

Whether you know it or not, you are already educating families. Every time you tell a family about what happened at school today, send home a piece of artwork, or sit down for a parent-teacher conference, your knowledge helps shape how the family thinks about their child. But you can go beyond these conversations in educating families, and create a wide variety of opportunities to expand their understanding of resilience.

Family Handbook

Your handbook is where you tell families what your school believes and values. In the sections in your handbook where you talk about what children learn at your school, make sure you include a discussion about the ways in which you support and teach resilience. If your school believes in teaching resilience, you should describe it in as much detail as you describe your approach to teaching literacy or conflict resolution.

In addition, your handbook probably has a significant section on health and safety, describing various policies and procedures. Resilience can feature prominently here as well, since the concepts are closely related. Consider a health and safety section like this one from the handbook at my school, the Children's Community School in Philadelphia:

> CCS takes children's health very seriously. We strive always to keep children safe from injury and disease. At the same time, we recognize that all children sometimes get hurt or sick in the normal course of development. We believe a healthy child is a child who can recover from life's inevitable setbacks. To that end, we take specific steps to prevent and reduce illness; to prevent and reduce injury; and to foster and increase children's resilience.
>
> To prevent and reduce illness, we [exclude ill children from our program, bleach our tables, teach children to wash hands carefully, etc.]

To prevent and reduce injury, we [supervise children carefully during play, provide developmentally appropriate materials and structures for physical play, teach children self-care skills, etc.]

To foster and increase children's resilience, we [encourage thoughtful risk taking in play, teach children to be active in their own recovery from injuries, etc.]

A section like this not only makes your health and safety policies and practices clear but also places them in the context of social and emotional learning and your school's values.

Documentation

Anytime you're creating a record of what happens at your school in order to tell a story about it, you're making documentation. Documentation could be a panel you make and hang on the wall of your classroom; it could also be a display of children's artwork, an e-mail to families about what happened at school today, a blog post about a particular classroom practice, or any of a hundred other things. Any context in which you're sharing artwork or photos or anecdotes is documentation, and anyplace you use documentation is a place to talk about resilience.

Do you make documentation panels to hang on your school's walls? Make one about adventurous play the children engage in, and show how it builds resilience. For example, photos of children climbing up the outside of the climbing structure could be posted with text saying, "When children push themselves to take reasonable risks, they build self-confidence and the ability to recover when things go wrong!"

Do you write daily e-mail messages to families about what happened at school or send a weekly newsletter? Don't just write about literacy and math; include pieces about physical and social and emotional learning. "Today at school many of the children worked together to build an obstacle course in the yard, and then raced to see who could get through it fastest! There were a few falls and bumps along the way, but the friendly teamwork atmosphere encouraged children to quickly get back up and keep working. What great recovery skills these kids have!"

Do you write blog posts about your school's practices? Write one about how teachers respond to injuries, emphasizing the idea that injuries are learning opportunities. "Earlier this week I was out in the yard when a child tripped and fell, and I had the pleasure of observing the wonderful support Teacher Jordan gave. Here's what she did . . ."

In general, think back to the idea of advertising and selling. How can you show people the great practices at your school? How can you show them just how great those practices are?

Workshops

If your school already holds workshops for families, you know that they can be wonderful contexts for interested families to benefit from teachers' expertise in a structured way. If you don't hold workshops for families, think how much the children in your program could benefit from even limited, easy-to-plan workshops, such as Five Things You Can Do at Home to Support Literacy or Learning Math in Everyday Life. Families are usually eager to learn schools' approaches to trickier topics as well; the workshops I do at school every year on positive discipline always play to a standing-room-only crowd.

A workshop on helping children become resilient would be very appealing to many families. Families often have to deal with children who have dramatic reactions to frustrations, disappointments, and injuries, and they tend to be eager for strategies to help their children recover more gracefully. Share your school's approaches to risk taking, injury, relationships, and safety. Families will thank you, and it'll help the children too. Look back at the perspectives in chapter 2 and the strategies in chapter 3; many of them can easily be shifted from the context of a school to that of a family and would make great material for a workshop. For a sample outline you could use to run a workshop for families, see appendix A.

Invite Families In

If you really want families to learn about your practice, just hearing about it is not enough. Like children, families learn best from seeing real-life modeling and getting hands-on, trial-and-error experience. The best way to provide this exposure is to invite families into your classroom during regular school days.

Many teachers don't like having family members in the room; they feel scrutinized or judged, as if they need to do everything perfectly. Believe it or not, many families feel the same way every day at drop-off and pickup times, when we see them parenting for all of five minutes—they're worried we'll see them being bad parents! If we allow families to come and see what we do— and even see our mistakes—they'll feel more connected to us, more confident in what we do, and better able to do what *they* do. I've had parents in my class-room on crazy days, when I felt like I was barely staying above water, only to have them approach me at the end of the day to say, "I learned so much from how you handled things!" Families in your classroom are not a threat; they're an opportunity for communication and education.

One easy way to start having families around is to ask for volunteers for specific projects during school hours.[6] Ask for someone to help with a cook-ing or art project, and give them specific jobs and instructions. ("Thanks for coming in! I'm going to have you take dictation for kids' stories. You sit here, and when children finish a drawing I'll send them to you, and you can write down what they say about it on the back.") While this adult is working on the specific project, they'll also have a chance to watch the rest of the classroom and see how you interact with children—how you help resolve conflicts, how you react to injuries, how you supervise children at play. Just seeing you in action will give them a great idea of your approach.

In addition to invitations to volunteer, you can open your doors to family members who want to watch and learn. Give them a good vantage point to watch from, and some tips on effective observation ("If a child comes over to talk to you, you can smile and say, 'I'm just watching today.'") When parents are observing in my classroom, I'll often stand next to them and narrate what I'm seeing and thinking, so that they can access my perspective. "Look how high Amelia's climbed on the jungle gym! She's been working hard on climb-ing as high as the older kids. Oh, now she looks a little scared. I'm going to

---

6 Unfortunately, many families do not have schedules that allow them to visit school during the day. Whenever you create opportunities for families to participate at school, it's important for families who work not to feel excluded. Offer opportunities for volunteering, participating, and learning in the evening or on weekends to be as accessible as possible to all families. Though you can only offer on-the-floor modeling and coaching in resilience if they come while you're teaching, other kinds of learning work too, and give more families the benefit of your expertise.

REFLECTION

Complete this sentence: "I wish families at our school had a better understanding of _____." What are ways you've already tried to communicate about that issue? What are ways you *could* be communicating about it?

go stand next to her and encourage her, but I won't lift her down—I want her to know that she can do it herself."

In both these approaches, you're modeling, just as you do for children; once again, good educational approaches work at all ages. As families see the real-life ways you support resilience in children, they'll be able to understand and apply your approaches much better.

Building a Culture of Resilience

This chapter has described a variety of tools and practices to work with families on building resilience in children—ways to build trusting relationships with families; ways to effectively communicate about your practices around resilience, health, and safety; ways to educate families about your approaches. Taken together, these strategies and approaches help create a school culture of resilience.

A culture is a set of shared values, expectations, and practices within a community. The approaches in this chapter can help the families you work with place value on children's long-term growth and development and on building their resilience. They can help families expect their children to be active and physical; to know that children learn and develop in physical ways; and to anticipate that children will sometimes get injured in the normal course of development. Families will trust teachers to care for their children and actively communicate with staff about safety, risk, and resilience.

When the families you work with, as a group, share these values, expectations, and practices, you'll know that resilience is part of your school culture. Culture affects everyone who is a part of it, so positive changes you help families make will become positive changes for their children as well. As resilience becomes a great part of the culture families experience, so it also will be reinforced for the children with whom you work.

~ 5 ~

Working with Teachers

Let's start with a story.

Sabot at Stony Point is a preschool–middle school in Richmond, Virginia. Over ten years ago, they decided they needed to start taking advantage of a small "wild space" that their campus bordered. *We know that spending time in the woods will be good for children*, they said to themselves, *so we had better figure out how to do it.* A few years later, they moved to a new site across the street from Larus Park, a one-hundred-acre forest, in which they created an outdoor classroom and daily explorations for all ages.

When this new aspect of the school's programming started, some staff members were eager to take children into the woods; others were understandably reluctant. Teachers worried about logistics—what if someone needs to go to the bathroom? They worried about boundaries—how will the children know how far is too far? They worried about physical discomfort—the children's and their own. And of course, they worried about safety—the forest is home to yellow jackets, copperhead snakes, sharp sticks, logs to fall off, hidden rocks, and so on.

Ten years later, the forest is an integral part of Sabot's programming. It offers nonstop opportunities for teaching and learning about problem solving, community, science, and, of course, resilience. But the changes the teachers had to make, to their ideas and their practices, were substantial. How did Sabot successfully make these changes?

This chapter explores strategies for educators for working on issues of resilience. You may be a director trying to encourage your reluctant staff to allow more rough-and-tumble play at school. You may be a teacher getting looks from your colleagues when you let children hang from their knees on the monkey bars. You may be a consultant or teacher trainer trying to convince teachers that health doesn't begin and end with injury prevention. Whatever your situation, you may find yourself in the position of trying to change ideas and practices connected to active physical play, risk, injury, and resilience.

There are many reasons to pursue change in other teachers. On the most basic level, it's hard to implement practices yourself if those around you aren't supportive. The perceptions of our colleagues matter: we all have a deep need to be respected and to be seen as caring and competent. If you're doing your best to support resilience but those around you misperceive your practice as endangering children, it's not going to go well for any of you. It's more effective, and less stressful, to work in a community where our colleagues support us and share similar practices and values.

Beyond that, we care what other teachers do. We want what's best for all children, so it matters to us how other teachers are teaching. We care about the practices at our schools and in our communities, and we want the field as a whole to be doing the best work it can. We need to communicate our understanding of best practices to the professionals with whom we're connected. If you care about building children's resilience, you'll want to work with your colleagues to help them see things the same way.

But change is difficult for anyone, and getting other people to change is even harder. It's important to be able to think about the process of change and see strategies that will help. Let's look at what the process of change at Sabot at Stony Point entailed for individuals and for the school.

Elaine Phillips, a preschool teacher at Sabot, is an outdoorsy person who found herself afraid of the possibilities that came with taking children to the woods. She worried about the lack of organization and control inherent in spending time in the woods and what it would mean for her ability to meet her students' needs. Her coteacher, who helped her create strategies to meet children's needs in the woods, supported her. "It helps to have a partner who's comfortable with risks," Elaine says. The growth mind-set ingrained in the school's culture also supported her: at Sabot, all teachers see themselves as learners, and Elaine remembers saying to herself, "I can learn this."

Other teachers I talked to at the school reported being simply unwilling to take children to the woods at first, out of concern for children's safety. Far from insisting that these teachers go outside their comfort zones, colleagues respected one another's boundaries, and since no one felt pressured, tensions around the new practice stayed low. But as more and more teachers started taking students to the woods, others sensed, as one told me, "the train was leaving the station." Beyond that, Sabot's culture involves a great deal of documentation, and teachers could see concrete evidence of the amazing learning that was taking place in the woods. In ongoing conversations with supportive colleagues, teachers who weren't participating would hear about others' successes and start to see the learning opportunities their students were missing by not going to the woods. Over the first few years, almost all the teachers were trying out the woods and finding success there.

Irene Carney, the director at Sabot, describes the process of changing teaching practices as very long. There were many staff meetings, casual conversations, school policies, and *lots* of problem solving around the practicalities of this new program, as well as the benefits it held. In particular, she says, when teachers were reluctant she asked them to articulate precisely what their concerns were. Each concern, once articulated, could be discussed and addressed by the group working together.

Irene also mentioned the importance of letting people take "baby steps"—for instance, a reticent teacher might read and draw at the edge of the woods with one group of children while another group went deeper in. Several teachers told me that little "tastes" allowed them to compare their expectations of the woods with reality. As mentioned in chapter 2 (see "Children as Risk Takers: What's Realistic?"), preschool teacher Nancy Sowder articulated early fears that, without the boundaries of fences, teachers would lose control of children. But when they tried it out, they found that their expectations were unrealistic, and that in the unbounded space of the woods children naturally regulated themselves and changed their behavior to match the environment. Another preschool teacher there told me, "Children slow *way* down when they start. Being in the forest brings out community and connection, caretaking." The teachers all discovered that their fears were unfounded: far from children getting wild in the woods, the wild space brought out children's kindness and patience and care with each other. As teachers felt empowered to try out the woods, without pressure, they could see what fears were realistic and what opportunities they hadn't thought of.

As a leader at the school while they approached this big transition, Irene recognized that change is always hard and didn't try to rush it. Indeed, the process of incorporating the forest into the school's practice isn't complete, she says—ten years on, there are teachers who are still figuring out what practices work and how to be comfortable. But the school as a whole has worked together to build a practice and a culture, and now the forest is part of the school's identity.

Our goal in this book is to help teachers and schools build an integrated understanding and practice around resilience. We want to help teachers see active play and physical risk and resilience as important parts of children's development and learning, and we want to support them in building practices that promote resilience. We want teachers to feel supported in their choices and explorations regarding resilience and that they are seen as trusted, valued professionals. We want to build a professional community that promotes resilience in children and adults alike. As we discuss strategies to support the changes reaching for this goal entails, we'll look to the story of Sabot at Stony Point as an example of what a successful process of change can look like.

Work with Yourself

Most of this chapter will be about asking others to change their ideas and practices. But if you want to successfully work with others, you've got to work with yourself first. You need to make sure you're not asking others to do things you're not willing to do yourself. More important, you're going to be asking teachers to work in some areas that may be emotionally charged—their identities as teachers, their beliefs about what's best for children, their own experiences with safety and risk, and so on—so you'll need to be prepared to have some serious conversations.

Take the time to ask yourself about your own beliefs, values, and biases around the topics of this book. Look back at the questions at the very beginning of chapter 1 and think about your experiences with physical play, risk, and injury when you were a child, in your adult life, and in your teaching experience. How have those experiences influenced how you interact with children's physical development and play?

Think, too, about your broader teaching experience. What's important to you in a child's development? What's your personal philosophy of what makes a good education? How do you understand children's learning, and what do you think makes good teaching? And how does the idea of resilience fit into your broader understanding of children's needs?

Finally, take some time to watch children at play, and attend to your own responses to what you see. What parts of children's play make you excited? What parts make you nervous? What's your immediate gut reaction when you see a child get hurt, or when you see a near miss?

Taking a thorough inventory of how you feel will allow you to communicate more clearly and honestly with other teachers, and communication will be an important part of making successful, sustainable change.

You may find, as you investigate your own perspectives, that you have some internal conflict concerning resilience. For instance, you may believe intellectually that allowing risk taking is valuable, but when you see a child hanging upside down you can't stop yourself from running to her side. That's okay! These are complicated issues, and it's appropriate for feelings and ideas to be complicated. Feeling ambivalent doesn't mean you should stop exploring; it means you should explore thoughtfully and carefully. Try something out, see how it goes, and reflect on how it connects to your core beliefs and practices. Change takes time, but attending thoughtfully to the process will get you there in the end.

Asking for Change

You're going to be asking teachers to make changes—in their practices (such as, "Let's start allowing children to roughhouse") and in their ideas (for example, "Let's keep in mind the potential benefits of injury"). As I'm sure you know, any kind of change—even positive, desired change—is stressful and takes work. Robert Evans (more on him in a moment) points out that resistance to change is a normal part of the change process. "Though we exalt [change] in principle," he writes, "we oppose it in practice. Most of us resist it whenever it comes upon us. We dislike alterations in even our smallest daily routines, such as a highway improvement detour on our route to work, for example, let alone in the larger aspects of our life and career, such as a major restructuring of our workplace" (Evans 2001). Trying to create change in an organization—for instance, getting the staff of a school, all of whom have existing practices and perspectives, to change the school's culture to include resilience as a value—is an enormous task.

Why is asking for change so difficult? Why can't we just tell teachers good ideas, and trust teachers—who are, as a group, dedicated, conscientious, and thoughtful—to implement those good ideas? Why can't you just hand every teacher at a school a copy of this book and expect practices to change accordingly?[1]

Evans is a consultant who works especially with schools on implementing reform, and he writes that change "provokes loss, challenges competence, creates confusion, and causes conflict" (2001, 21). Change provokes loss because teachers must let go of principles, practices, and habits that they've built up over time and that they've invested in, professionally and emotionally. Change challenges competence, because teachers are being told the way they're used to doing things isn't good enough, and the new ways are unfamiliar. Change creates confusion, because expectations are no longer familiar and comfortable. Change causes conflict, because a change will always work out better, or at least be more comfortable, for some people than for others. In other words, when asking teachers to make changes, we need to be mindful that even the most positive of changes can represent a hardship or threat.

In addition, as the person asking for the change ("Hey everyone, let's incorporate a focus on resilience into our practice!"), you are in a particular position. If you've read this far in the book and are considering how to ask successfully for change in teachers, I'll assume that you're at least somewhat on board with the ideas here. Perhaps you've already started to incorporate some of the strategies in this book into your practice and have made changes to your way of doing things. That means you're coming from a different place than are many of the teachers you'll be talking to, who haven't necessarily even considered these ideas. Evans writes, "Reformers who press staff to innovate have already assimilated the reform and found their own meaning in it. They have already worked out a reformulation of purposes and practices that makes sense to them, which may have taken them months or years to accomplish" (2001, 63). In other words, your journey has already involved time and energy; you need to leave space for other teachers to take that time and energy as well.

Recognize that even the best ideas in the world can't be sustainably implemented by decree. Education is a relationship-based practice, and the people involved—children, families, and *teachers*—all have needs. Change isn't a

---

1   However, if you *want* to buy a copy of this book for everyone on your staff, please don't let me stop you!

rational, predictable, controllable process that you can plan out from beginning to end; it's a relational, uncertain, emergent process that will depend on everyone's input throughout changing circumstances.

Change is a complicated process, and there's no recipe for making changes successfully. That said, there are some things that will be necessary parts of your process:

- **Time.** Rome wasn't built in a day; incorporating resilience fully into a caregiver's practice won't happen in a week, a month, or even a year. As we saw in the story of Sabot's development, some of these changes can take a decade or more. So be patient!

- **Work.** There's no magic wand to wave. Incorporating resilience fully into practice will take some effort—on your part and teachers'. Plan to put some effort in, and be mindful that you'll be asking others to do work as well.

- **Mutuality.** Change is a two-way street. As we've discussed, if you want others to change, you need to be prepared to make changes yourself.

- **Trust.** For someone to be ready to make a change you're asking for, they need to trust that you know them and understand them. For them to trust you, they need to know that you trust them. Trust creates the sense of safety and value that makes people feel ready to take the risks, and put in the work required for change.

- **Relationships.** Trust arises out of relationships, which are also necessary to change. Someone walking in and asking for change on her first day will probably not be welcomed with open arms. Take the time to make real connections before you start asking people to enter a process that will take work and time and trust.

- **Communication.** Trusting relationships are built on communication. You've heard this before, and you know where this is going . . .

. . . because the principles of working with teachers are going to be the same as the principles we discussed for working with families and with children. Many of these practices will sound very familiar.

One way to approach change with adults is to think about how you approach change with children. You have to be just as supportive and patient and kind with colleagues. Of course you shouldn't condescend to adults, any more than you would take a condescending attitude toward a child. Rather, remember that we are all people, and we all need support and scaffolding. A new practice is challenging and scary. You never want to push someone to a place where the person is uncomfortable, just as you would never push a child into something the child is scared of. Think of the support and understanding you give to children when they're trying something new, and offer the same level of support and understanding to adults.

> **REFLECTION**
>
> Think of a time someone asked you to make a change in your practice. How did that experience feel to you? If it was a positive experience, what made it work so well? If it was a negative experience, what could have made it better?

Changing Teachers' Ideas

Asking teachers to incorporate resilience (or any new concept) into their teaching is a question of asking them to change their thinking. You might be asking teachers to *add* new ideas to what they already know—for instance, adding "resilience" to a list of skills to teach that already includes things like reading and conflict resolution. You might be asking them to *reprioritize* existing values—for instance, seeing resilience as more important or urgent than reading. You might be asking them to change how they look at certain situations, to use the lens of resilience to *reframe* their everyday experiences— for instance, approaching a child throwing rocks not from a "safety first" perspective but from a "this is an opportunity to learn about making choices" perspective.

A big part of your success in the long, gradual process of changing teachers' ideas will depend on your ability to communicate clearly. Strategies for effective communication with families apply equally well to communication with teachers. To build the trusting relationships that come from good communication, you'll need to be good at both talking and listening. You'll need to express your own values and practices clearly, while actively making space for dialogue and soliciting input from others. Those approaches are all covered in much more depth in chapter 4—but there are also some things to keep in mind that apply specifically to dialogue with colleagues.

You'll be most effective in changing ideas if you create opportunities for multiple conversations, over time, at many different scales. An all-staff meeting about resilience is probably an important part of your process, but by itself it won't change your school's culture. Large-group conversations are useful for getting ideas out there, but small-group conversations are where ideas can shift more productively. Resilience is an important topic for team meetings, where everyone has space to speak up among the people they work with most closely. One-on-one conversations are important too: check in with individual teachers about how they feel about the ideas and the process of change, and give them an opportunity to voice both successes and concerns.

Dialogue shouldn't always be formal, though. Meetings with agendas are incredibly useful, but casual "how's it going, what's on your mind" conversations are also an important part of effective communication. A casual conversation can be a space for ideas to move incrementally—as opposed to a set meeting with an agenda, where people can feel pressure to be "right." Consider bringing up resilience during low-key times (for instance, on the playground, where there are often concrete examples to discuss!).

Remember, too, that dialogue can't and shouldn't depend solely on you. In the same way that children's learning is most effective when children speak directly to each other instead of always to or through a teacher, staff's dialogue will be most effective if some of it happens without you there. No matter how welcoming of dissent you are, if you're asking for change, your colleagues will always perceive that there is a "right answer" when you're in the room. Encourage teachers to discuss resilience without you so that they have opportunities to share ideas without an authority figure listening. Honest dialogue without you will encourage honest dialogue *with* you.

Conversations about change can sometimes get stuck in the realm of opinions: "Well, I think *X*, and you think *Y*—I guess we'll just agree to disagree." It helps to have some external content to discuss. Find a thought-provoking article, book chapter, or blog post to mull over together (see appendix B for some possibilities). Watch a video together of a teacher supporting resilience and share thoughts. Visit a school with an existing practice that promotes resilience to see these ideas in action. Having something external to refer to will help ensure everyone is talking about the same thing, and give a frame to help articulate thoughts and feelings.

Throughout your process of change, make sure to help everyone find the common ground that connects you. Frame a larger conversation about what you all agree on—what children need, for instance, or what it means to be a professional in early childhood, or what the mission of your school is. By couching the conversation about resilience in the context of shared beliefs and values, teachers will be better able to see each other's points of view. When disagreements inevitably arise, it will be easier to disagree respectfully and find a road map to resolution.

When an honest, ongoing dialogue is a part of your process, you reinforce the trusting relationships that are a necessary part of successful change.

Changing Teaching Practices

Changing teachers' ideas about resilience is both important and difficult—but changing teachers' practices is a whole nother kettle of fish. A lot of teaching practice, particularly the moment-to-moment stuff, operates on instinct: we react to what we see right in front of us, often without conscious intent. Even the best teachers rely on habits—habits created over years of thoughtful, intentional practice, but habits nonetheless. Habits are very difficult to change without hard work, time, and support. When you're trying to change teaching practices, here are some strategies that can help. (Note: These strategies are all described as though you're trying to change the practices of a teaching staff you supervise, but they're also effective if you're trying to change your own teaching practices.)

Address Fears and Provide Safety

Fear is bad for learning. As we discussed in chapter 3, if children feel unsafe, they can't learn effectively. The same is true for adults: if teachers feel unsafe, they won't be able to develop new practices. There are many reasons a new practice around resilience might make teachers feel afraid or unsafe. At Sabot they spent lots of time getting teachers to articulate their fears about the forest practice, so that fears could be adequately addressed. As you push teachers to change practices to incorporate a focus on resilience, take the time to find out what aspects cause anxiety for them, and provide support for those needs.

Here are some concerns teachers might have, and the beginnings of responses that might help:

IF TEACHERS SAY . . .	YOU MIGHT START BY SAYING . . .
"I'm worried children will get hurt."	"Let's map out some clear rules for play together that will let children explore but still let you feel comfortable."
"I'm worried that children will get hurt, and then my supervisor won't trust me to keep children safe."	"I am entirely confident that you have children's best interests at heart—but safety isn't children's only interest. As we figure out how to balance multiple needs, I'll be right there with you."
"I'm worried that children will get hurt, and then their families will be upset with me."	"The school knows and has evidence that you are a trustworthy teacher; in any dispute with a parent about safety the school will have your back." (More on this below.)
"I'm worried that I won't be as good a teacher in this new system."	"The school doesn't expect perfection from you any more than you expect perfection from children; what we value is learning and growth, and we're going to do it together."

If teachers feel comfortable enough to take risks in their practice, they'll be able to change and learn. But their comfort level depends on the support and communication you give them.

Take Baby Steps

As the teachers at Sabot realized, trying to institute big changes all at once wouldn't have worked very well. If they had said, "Starting next week, all classes will spend three hours in the woods every week," they would have scared a lot of teachers (and children!) and generated a lot of resistance. Start with small, achievable changes to practice and work your way up. Set teachers up for success, just the way you do with children. You don't start a two-year-old on the forty-eight-piece jigsaw puzzle; you start her on the four-piece puzzle with the nice grabby knobs and give her gradually harder puzzles as her skills grow. Similarly, don't force a teacher to jump straight into allowing roughhousing in class; start with an achievable change, such as, "If you see a child fall down in the gym, wait to see if he cries before you go over to help." Then, when and if that practice seems to be working well, ask for another incremental change. Let small successes build up to bigger ones.

Find Middle Ground

You may try to implement a particular practice connected to building resilience—"We're going to allow children to climb on the outside of the climbing structure"—and encounter reluctance from teachers. Remember that the goal isn't any particular teaching practice, but rather a school culture that values and supports resilience. So don't insist on a certain rule or practice that makes some teachers feel too uncomfortable; find a middle ground that works for everyone. Try these strategies:

- **Find a compromise.** "Some teachers feel it's not safe for children to climb on the outside of the structure. How about we allow them to climb up the slide, but not the outside of the climber?"

- **Refine the practice.** "Some teachers are worried about children falling off the climber. What about a new rule that children can climb on the outside of the structure only if a teacher is standing next to them?"

- **Tolerate differences.** You don't need to insist on a school-wide rule; it's okay for different teachers to have different practices. I used to work at a school where children knew that different teachers had different comfort levels with risk taking. I might tell a child, "Please don't climb there. I'm worried you'll fall." "But Teacher Sara lets me climb here!" "Teacher Sara is more comfortable with risks than I am. While I'm here it's my job to make sure I feel children are safe, so I'm asking you to come down. When Teacher Sara is here, you can climb here." The children had no difficulty understanding the system and adjusting their behavior accordingly when the system was clearly articulated.

Remember that change is a gradual process, and small changes eventually add up to big changes. Make a small change that teachers can feel comfortable with, and build from there.

Provide Positive Reinforcement

Positive reinforcement is an important part of children's learning, and it is no less important for adults' learning. When teachers are successful in supporting children's resilience, it helps to provide reinforcement for that experience. Even more than reinforcing successes, per se, it's important to reinforce growth and change. When you see a teacher making an effort, or trying something new, it's important to tell them, "Good job!"

Well . . . not exactly, right? As we know from working with children, praise like *"Good job"* isn't the most effective reinforcement—among other problems, praise is an extrinsic reward that usually doesn't lead to internal change. Furthermore, adults often feel that straight-up praise is patronizing, especially when it's for something they didn't have full control over ("Good job complying with my instructions!"). If we want teachers to change practice for the long haul, we need better methods of reinforcement.

Just like with children, recognition and attention can be more effective than praise. To a child building confidence in climbing up the slide, you might say, "Betsy, I saw you climbing up the slide! You're really trying new things, aren't you?" To a teacher building a practice around resilience, you might say, "I noticed how you held back and let Betsy climb up the slide instead of lifting her down. That's different from how you would have done it a month ago, isn't it?"

Just like with children, an invitation to discuss the experience can be powerful reinforcement. With that same child, you might say, "Betsy, how did it feel to climb so high?" With that same teacher, you might say, "What were you thinking about while Betsy was climbing?"

And just like with children, the most effective reinforcement can be to call attention to their own experiences, so that they can ultimately reinforce themselves. To the child, "Betsy, you have such a big smile on your face every time you climb up that slide. It must make you feel really good!" To the teacher, "It's obvious you're working hard to implement the perspectives we've been talking about. Does it feel as successful as it looks?"

Note that every type of positive reinforcement (even praise) depends on having excellent supervision. You can't reinforce a behavior you didn't see. When you're asking teachers to make this kind of change, make a point of being around to watch them at work, so that you can "catch them being good."

Look for Results

Perhaps the most important positive reinforcement for teachers is to see that what they're doing is working. If teachers can tell that children are actually building resilience based on their efforts, it helps a lot. Even enthusiastic teachers need to see that what they're doing is worthwhile; teachers who are anxious about or skeptical of the new practices especially need to see results.

Part of your job can be to point out the effect the new practices are having on children. "Teacher John, I was watching after Emma scraped her knee, and you helped her recover. I noticed that you did what we'd been discussing—you asked Emma what she wanted to do to feel better, and she jumped up and said she wanted to keep playing. That moment really made a difference for her—I could tell how confident you made her feel."

It can also be powerful to get teachers to notice the results themselves. "Your class has been trying the new rules on the slide all week. Have you seen any changes in the children?" It can be even more effective to get teachers to notice successes in each other. Seeing the results of your own practice when you're right in the middle of it can be difficult, and a peer's perspective can be powerful. "Teacher Laurence, Teacher Sue has been working on implementing the strategies for responding to injuries. Have you seen any effect on the children when she tries the new approach?" A team meeting or staff meeting can be an excellent time to get teachers to point out one another's successes.

Form a Community of Practice

Anyone who's ever tried to make a change in his teaching practice without the support and participation of colleagues knows: it's really hard. No matter how much you believe in the importance of a new practice, if you're trying to implement it alone you're going to have a tough time of it. Doing what you've always done is easier than changing. You need the support of those around you if you're going to make a change and see it through.

A sense of shared values and practices is an immense support when making change. Sharing is helpful when things are going well—there's nothing like celebrating successes together for positive reinforcement! Sharing is also helpful when there are struggles—colleagues can offer sympathy, solidarity, and constructive ideas. At every point in the process of change, it helps to know that you're not going it alone.

Look back at the story of Sabot at Stony Point and notice how much of their process of change was about supporting each other and building community. They built new practices collaboratively and solved problems as a group through ongoing dialogue. They tied the changes to their shared values, such as the culture of growth at the school. They respected the needs of individuals and turned to each other for support when needed. The process of change at Sabot built a community of practice among the teachers, changing the culture and the identity of the school together.

A community of practice doesn't have to be the staff at a single school. Consider the powerful community of practice formed in a practicum class for student teachers—they get together regularly to discuss successes and challenges, to consider new approaches, and to offer mutual support. You can create the same kind of environment in many ways. If you go to a workshop on resilience, stay in touch with the other attendees through an e-mail list or conference calls. If you're interested in making a change in your own practice, post a notice on a local professional message board for people who are seeking similar changes and meet monthly to talk and provide support. Whether you're making a change yourself or helping others make a change, don't underestimate the importance of community.

REFLECTION

Think of teachers you know, at your school or elsewhere. Who might be open to exploring the ideas in this book? How might you start to create a community of practice with those teachers? Who are some teachers you think might have a hard time with these ideas? How might you begin to open a dialogue with them?

Building Resilience in Adults (and in Yourself)

Like any process of change, building a practice around resilience entails both successes and failures, learning and frustration, setbacks and steps forward. What teachers need to negotiate this process of ups and downs is, of course, *resilience*—the ability to bounce back from life's upsets. Whether you're supporting a staff you supervise or working with teacher peers or simply trying to develop yourself, you'll need to take the perspectives and techniques we've discussed for building resilience in children and apply them to adults.

Keep in mind, too, that whatever we want to teach children we have to know ourselves. If you want to teach children to read, it helps if you know how to read, and it helps even more if you love to read. If you want children to learn to cooperate, they need to see models of cooperation in their teachers and caregivers. And if we want teachers to support children's resilience, we'll need to help their teachers to be resilient themselves.

Let's review a couple of themes that came up in previous chapters and see how they might apply to teachers.

Risk

Risk is the possibility that something bad will happen as well as the possibility that something good will happen, and it's a crucial part of learning. If you want teachers to develop a new practice, they're going to have to take risks. Give them permission to try things and permission to fail. Let teachers know that you care more about their learning and growth than about their getting everything right the first time around. Let them know that they won't be penalized for trying to support children's resilience, even if it's not working out yet. And, as mentioned earlier, provide positive reinforcement when a teacher tries something new, whether it results in success or failure.

Here are ways you can support positive risk taking in teachers, borrowed from practices we've discussed for supporting children:

- **Supervise risk taking** (see chapter 2, "Harm Reduction"). Watch teachers as they work with children and provide them with constructive feedback and support.

- **Build self-confidence** (see chapter 3, "Building the Self Skills"). Encourage and recognize teachers for successes, and build positive relationships around practice.

- **Provide a range of risks to choose from** (see chapter 3, "Create an Environment for Joy and Learning" and "Building the Self Skills"). Find middle ground for new practices.

- **Connect risks to existing interests** (see chapter 3, "Calibrating Risk for Different Children"). Find connections between a teacher's existing values and resilience.

Injury

Okay, not injury exactly—it's pretty unlikely that a teacher will get injured through these practices, even if they're roughhousing with children (which I strongly encourage). But let's think about the adult analogue. For children, injury is the result of failing at something risky. When adults fail at something risky, we just call it "failure," but it can have a lot of injurious consequences: embarrassment, fear, frustration, reduction of self-confidence, and so on. Any of these "injuries" makes it harder for teachers to continue to learn. Just like with children, you don't want the experience of failure to be the wrong kind of learning experience, the kind that teaches you "I can't do it" or "Trying is scary" or "I'm not safe" (see chapter 3, "Responding to Injuries").

As with children, your response to failure should be calibrated to empower teachers, to make them feel that trying again is worthwhile. When children get injured, we respond with patient waiting and listening, balancing a message of trust and support and offering empowerment. We can offer the same respect and support to teachers, in an age-appropriate way. When a teacher tries a new practice and fails, try using phrases like the following:

- "It seemed like that didn't go the way you were hoping. Do you want to talk about it?"

- "Tell me more about what happened. What was going on for you in that moment?"

- "This is a tricky process, but I trust you. What do you want to do next time so that it turns out differently?"

Notice that none of those phrases involves telling a teacher how to solve the problem. In the same way that we want to empower children to choose the manner of recovery, we want teachers to have a sense of ownership in how they address and solve problems in their practice around building resilience.

Keep in mind, though, that adults are often much more defensive than children. If you wait for them to come to you with their failures, most never will. While most children bring a scraped knee straight to the nearest adult, teachers generally won't come to the director's office to say, "I really screwed up today." Part of being able to support teachers in dealing with failures requires, once again, high-quality supervision. If you're there to see teachers in action, you can see what's going on and offer a kind, "That seemed like a rough moment! I'll come check in with you later today, and we can problem solve together."

Trusting Relationships

We talked in chapter 3 about trusting children—trusting that they are capable of knowing and meeting their own needs, trusting that they want to learn and grow, trusting that injuries are not disasters. You need to trust teachers in the same way. Teachers want to teach as well as possible, and they will work hard to do so. They can tolerate some frustration and confusion and failure on the way to success. Even if a teaching practice isn't working today, it'll probably be better tomorrow. Trust teachers to be okay.

As in our work with families in chapter 4, trusting relationships are built from clear, two-way communication over time. Show teachers you trust them by really listening to what they have to say and honestly expressing your own perspectives and experiences. Build a long-term dialogue regarding issues of supporting children's resilience. Create a community of practice, in which teachers work together to incorporate change and support one another.

Trusting relationships are crucial to building resilience in children and to working with families. They're a vital part of building resilience in teachers as well.

Having Teachers' Backs

This chapter has been mostly about ways you can make teachers feel better about taking the risks associated with building a practice around resilience. But no matter what, you're still asking teachers to take risks, and by definition risks can have negative consequences. For teachers trying these new approaches, that might mean a child getting injured on their watch or a family becoming angry and distrustful toward them. It could also mean being a less successful teacher in the new system than the old. What you need to do, as someone asking teachers to take risks, is to assure them that, if the worst should happen, you've got their backs.

You can tell teachers, "I know how much you care for children. If a child you're supervising gets injured because you were letting her take a well-considered risk, you don't have to worry about what that means for you in your position at this school. An injury doesn't imply that you weren't doing your job." You can say, "If a family member has a problem with your resilience practice, you can send him straight to me. We know why this practice is important, and I am happy to talk about why we embrace this practice as a school and how your teaching practice is a part of our goals as a program. I will stand up for the quality of your teaching." You can tell them, "If you're having a hard time changing your practice, that's okay. Change is hard, and I'm not expecting or even looking for perfection. You won't be judged on how quickly you get things right; you'll be evaluated on your commitment to doing your best for children."

Of course, you can't offer blanket immunity for poor-quality care, especially when safety is involved. Offering teachers this level of trust and support requires you to know that their teaching merits it. Once again, vigilant supervision is the name of the game. You need to see teachers in action enough that you know their practice well. You need to work closely enough together that you know what choices they're making and why they're making them. You need to understand when a mistake happens just what that mistake means. You need to be ready to step in if a teacher isn't keeping children safe and to insist on improvement when it's needed.

When you truly know how your teachers teach, you can offer them an enormous amount of trust. That trust will let them trust you and help them do their jobs the very best that they can.

Building a Culture of Resilience

This chapter has described a number of ways to work with teachers on building resilience in children: ways to think about asking teachers for change and ways to value the changes that they make; ways to build dialogue around resilience; ways to support teachers in making gradual, achievable changes in practice; and ways to build resilience in teachers themselves. These approaches, together with the ideas throughout this book, help create a culture of resilience at your school—a set of shared values, expectations, and practices that apply to both children and adults.

In this framework, teachers value resilience in children, and children's long-term growth in general. We also value long-term growth for adults and believe that teaching is a profession of ongoing learning, where participation and cooperation are essential, and where resilience is seen as a crucial strength for adults as well as children.

We expect children to be active and physical and to learn and develop in physical ways, even if that sometimes results in injuries. Therefore, we expect that adults will work hard to find a balance in children's needs and offer the best holistic care possible. We expect that the process of learning to do this is long, ongoing, and full of both successes and failures.

We support teachers in developing practices to support children's resilience by building dialogue and communication; by learning through trial and error; by seeing teachers as learners who are offered just as much support for learning as children are. Through these values, expectations, and practices, we build a school culture in which resilience is valued and supported, for children and adults alike.

~ 6 ~

Licensing and Liability

If you run a school for young children, it will have already occurred to you that licensing and liability are important topics to think about when discussing building resilience in young children. In building children's resilience we are negotiating issues of safety, injury, and risk; licensing and liability are two frameworks that have a lot to say about these topics.

Every school is allowed to operate, in part, through the approval of a licensing agency. One of the primary concerns of licensing agencies is children's safety. Licensing agencies typically care much less about your terrific math curriculum and your engaging documentation practices than about whether you have covers on all the outlets and if there's an adequate fall zone around your climber. If a school isn't sufficiently providing for children's safety, the licensing agency could, potentially, close the school.

Liability, as a general definition, means being responsible for something. In our culture, we tend to use the word to mean being legally responsible for something. More particularly, we tend to mean, "You could be sued for this if you screw it up." A school is legally responsible for the children in its care and could, potentially, be sued if it negligently compromises the safety of those children.

Right there, in those short descriptions, are not just the reasons that licensing and liability are *important* to think about; they're why they are *scary* to think about. No one wants to think about getting shut down or sued. Even though those outcomes are extremely rare, the idea of them is a big concern for those who run schools.

It's important to acknowledge our fear. It's equally important not to let fear be our guiding principle. As we discussed in chapter 2, if we let fear of unlikely outcomes guide our practice, we end up taking more and more away from children. If we are guided by the question "What's the worst that could happen, and how can I make sure to avoid it?," we are led down a path that does not serve children or ultimately meet their needs. We need to ask ourselves these questions instead: What do we want for children? What are children's needs, and how can we meet them? How do we do what we know is best for children—including allowing them to take risks and sometimes even get injured—without letting our fears about licensing and liability drive our decision making? This chapter offers some frames for answering those questions.

It's important to note that I'm not in any way a legal expert. I'm sharing here strategies and perspectives that have worked for schools I've been a part of and for schools that have established practices around building resilience in young children. I am indebted particularly in this chapter to the wisdom and experience of Joan Symonds, director of the Children's Center at Diablo Valley College in Pleasant Hill, California; Irene Carney, the executive director of Sabot at Stony Point in Richmond, Virginia; and Belann Giaretto, the executive director of Pacific Primary School in San Francisco, California.

Licensing

It's easy to slip into an "us versus them" mind-set with regard to licensing. "We're trying to give kids cool opportunities, and licensing just keeps coming in and saying no!" We're the good guys, and they're the bad guys, right? But that perspective, while understandable, is neither true nor helpful. Caregivers and licensing consultants have important common ground: both are working to do what's best for children. They may have different ideas about what is best and how to achieve it, but the root goal is the same, and it's important.

It's also important to remember that licensing isn't a single, unitary, hegemonic institution. It's a collection of people doing their best to give children healthy, safe environments according to their agency's rules and priorities—which can sometimes be confusing or even conflicting—and their own best judgment. When we're having a conflict with "licensing," really we're having trouble problem solving with one or two individuals—one or two individuals who, like you, are trying to do what's best for children.

If you can shift your perspective on licensing to a framework of "we're working together to meet children's needs," you're going to be much more able to find productive ways to solve problems in ways that meet both licensing's requirements and your own standards of what quality early childhood education means.

Work within the Law

Licensing regulations govern the operation of your program. You must obey the relevant laws; that much is clear. That said, there are several useful ways to think about what it means to obey the law.

Obey the Letter of the Law

It is, of course, your responsibility to know what the licensing regulations say and to comply with them. Most of the time, licensing regulations are written clearly and are not, in truth, all that burdensome to meet. Yes, it's very frustrating when your licensing consultant tells you the kids can't use that rope swing anymore, and it's annoying to learn you'll have to buy mats for all the bathrooms to comply with nonslip regulations. But if you work proactively with licensing (more on that soon), you can address most problems before they come up. Problems that do arise are generally much more straightforward to address than substantive questions of practice, for example, "How can we better assess children?" or "How do we engage children in a productive exploration of race and differences?" (two questions my school has been grappling with recently while simultaneously opening a brand-new site, full of new licensing requirements).

It's important to remember you can do many amazing things in your program's environment, even given licensing requirements. Think of the environments at the best preschools you've ever observed at, the photos of inspiring playgrounds and gross-motor rooms in books about making great early childhood spaces[1]—all of those were created within in the bounds of licensing regulations. Even within the letter of the law, the sky's the limit.

Obey the Spirit of the Law

Licensing regulations are created for an important and positive purpose: to keep children safe. That works out great, because that's our job too. We may not always agree with regulations about what exactly safety means or how

---

1   See appendix B for recommendations.

best to achieve it, but we agree that safety is important. So while you're busy complying with the letter of the law, keep the spirit of the law in mind as well.

That means, to the best of your ability and understanding, keep children safe. You may believe (like I do) that fall-zone regulations aren't as important in preventing injuries as good supervision during climbing. Well then, be good about supervision while complying with fall-zone regulations. You may think (like I do) that the regulation about wearing helmets while riding trikes is unnecessary and that what's most important is teaching kids to look where they're going. You're still going to put helmets on them, because that's the rule, but you'll also teach them as well as you can to look where they're going.

In other words, in addition to complying with licensing's standards, live up to your own standards of what, in your understanding, constitutes adequate safety. When everyone is working conscientiously to ensure safety, not only will the children be best cared for, but also disagreements with licensing (keep reading) will be easier to resolve.

Collaborate with Licensing

Licensing is a collection of people working toward a goal you share. You can each best achieve your interpretation of that goal by working collaboratively *with* the other group.

Build Relationships

In many places, a program is inspected by the same licensing consultant again and again. If this is the case for you, you have an enormous opportunity to build a trusting, communicative, collaborative relationship. Just as we've discussed with children, families, and colleagues, strong relationships aren't built overnight—it takes communication and connection over time. You can make a commitment to kindly greeting and welcoming your consultant every time you see him or her. Instead of saying, "I'll talk with you when you're done," you can take the time to walk around the school with your consultant, asking about his or her perspective on what is seen and sharing things you're especially proud of. You can take the consultant's recommendations and requirements in the spirit in which they're intended—to benefit children—and work to solve problems together. Over time, you'll be able to build a relationship where both parties respect and understand the other.

Even if you don't see the same licensing consultant every time, you can still be kind and communicative to every new person you meet. And perhaps even if you see a different consultant at each in-person meeting, there might be someone in the licensing office you can speak with on the phone when questions or issues come up, and you can build a relationship with that person.

Communicate

As in your work with children, families, and colleagues, a huge part of working successfully with licensing involves honest, straightforward communication. If you can share your intentions with your licensing consultant, he or she will be more likely to be able to help you problem solve to accomplish your goals.

If licensing vetoes something you believe is good for children—say, a rope swing in your yard—active communication can be a tool for cooperative problem solving. "Hmm," you might say, "the rope swing has been such a great place for the children to work on taking turns and sharing, not to mention the great vestibular stimulation it gives them. We'd really hate to lose it entirely. Can you help me figure out a way to alter it so that it complies with licensing's requirements?"

Communication can go beyond reacting to problems as they come up; you can be proactive in your communication, reaching out to licensing before a problem exists. You can call your licensing consultant on the phone and say, "We're thinking about putting a rope swing in our yard, and we want to make sure we do it safely. Can you tell us what we need to know so that the swing will comply with regulations?" Proactive communication helps avoid problems; it also builds trust and collaboration. When the consultant comes to your site and sees the swing, you'll be able to honestly say, "Thank you so much for helping us make this happen! Look what joy and learning your input allowed us to create!"

An Example

My colleague Joan Symonds, director of the Children's Center at Diablo Valley College in Pleasant Hill, California, built a strong working relationship with her school's licensing consultant over several years. One spring the school installed a birdbath in the playground, and the children loved watching the birds from the windows of the classroom. It hadn't even occurred to Joan that the birdbath was something licensing would be concerned with. But when the consultant came, he told her that water features were considered drowning hazards, and the birdbath would have to be removed.

Instead of either complying or arguing, Joan drew on their positive working relationship and said, "Oh, that hadn't occurred to me, but I can see that perspective. The birdbath has been such a benefit to the children, though, really helping them connect with nature and science. Can we look together at the regulations and see if we can find a solution that will allow us to keep it?" As they looked through the regulations book together, the consultant pointed out that the regulations concerned the maximum depth of water containers over a certain size. After a bit of brainstorming, they hit on a solution of filling the bottom of the birdbath with smooth river stones from one of the classrooms so that the effective depth of the water would only be half an inch, which would still allow the birds to bathe. The solution met the letter of the law for licensing requirements, and it obeyed the spirit of the law by avoiding any significant danger to children. Furthermore, the solution was found via the positive, communicative relationship between the school's director and the licensing consultant.

░░░░░░░░░░░░░░░░░

The specifics of any set of licensing regulations will differ from state to state and city to city, as will the culture of particular licensing agencies. But if you can think of licensing as a group of reasonable people that share a common goal with you, you'll be able to work together to find solutions that meet children's needs. Your physical space can contain features that challenge children's bodies and allow productive risk taking—swings, bikes, exciting climbers, and beyond—it's just a matter of finding solutions together.

REFLECTION

What have been your experiences with licensing as an institution and with individual licensing consultants? If you have had positive experiences, what has made them so successful? If you have had negative experiences, what strategies do you think would be effective in improving your relationship with licensing?

Liability

The fear of lawsuits is real. Like licensing, it can be easy to see liability as something scary while overlooking its essentially positive nature. Schools are entrusted with children's welfare. If a school is negligent in that responsibility, it *should* have to answer for that. Legal liability exists in order to help ensure accountability and standards of safety; we can all agree that schools should, in fact, be accountable and safe.

Also like licensing, it can be burdensome to operate a facility under the looming specter of liability, but we can't allow fear of potential lawsuits to be our primary guide in decision making. Operating based on fear doesn't allow us to make the best choices for children. If we can reframe our approach to liability in terms of positive actions based on our values, we'll provide the best education for children.

Reduce Your Vulnerability to Lawsuits

There's a lot you can do as a school to make yourself less vulnerable to potential suits. Make sure you always *comply with licensing* so that all your practices are legally approved for children's safety. Do all you can to *supervise children well* so that serious injuries are unlikely. *Keep good records* of any incident and share that documentation with families when their children are hurt. These are all good, important practices in their own right; they're also practices that ensure your safety as a school. Don't provide opportunities for someone to take advantage of your lack of rigor.

Not only are these responsible practices; they are demonstrations of responsibility as well. Think back to the story from Sabot at Stony Point and the families' positive response to the lockdown (see "Communication" in chapter 4). Actions that clearly demonstrate the rigor of your safety procedures build families' trust in your program. If something small goes wrong later, families will be less likely to think it was because you were being negligent.

In addition, while the actions I've just described can help reduce your vulnerability to lawsuits, there's an important step to take to reduce the potential harm from a lawsuit: make sure you have adequate insurance. Talk to your insurer and confirm your coverage for financial damages, as well as legal and medical expenses. Make sure you ask, "What are we covered for if a child gets hurt? What are we covered for if we get sued?" In the unlikely and unpleasant event of a lawsuit, a good insurance policy can be the difference between your center's staying open and being forced to close.

Reduce Litigiousness

Reducing your vulnerability is only part of the picture. People don't bring lawsuits just because they can make a legal case. People bring lawsuits because something happened to make them feel angry, betrayed, or mistreated. Beyond demonstrating that you are keeping children safe and meeting your legal responsibilities, there's a lot you can do to minimize the feelings that lead to lawsuits. Take a look back at chapter 4, "Working with Families," and think about how the strategies and perspectives discussed in that chapter might help to reduce feelings of anger, even when something bad has happened.

The most important thing is to *build strong relationships* with the families you serve. When families feel connected to a school, and feel that the school is working together with them in the care of their children, they're more likely to understand and forgive when something goes wrong. A network of strong relationships builds a *community*, and communities care for each other. People generally don't sue people they care for; relationships and community help people work through problems and resolve conflicts together.

You build relationships through *good communication*. If you have a practice that includes clear communication, families will already know and understand your school's approach to caring for children and building resilience and will understand your point of view when a child gets hurt. Furthermore, if you've been communicating well, you'll be better at understanding the family's point of view and be able to more effectively meet their needs, even if their child has been hurt. Communication builds *trust*—trust that helps people see one another's good intentions and work together when something goes wrong.

Part of good communication is making sure you have *clear policies*. Look through your staff and family handbooks and make sure they clearly describe how teachers supervise play, the procedures for when a child gets hurt, and so on. And make sure, as best you can, that families actually take the time to read your policies. If families who disagree with your policies don't know what your policies are, they're likely to be surprised and angry when you put those policies into action. If instead your policies are clearly communicated from the outset, families can choose not to enroll.

Overall, though, if you create a school culture of resilience, everyone will have a shared understanding to rely on if a child gets hurt. When you share values and practices within a community, surprises are minimized and understanding is maximized.

Viewed through this lens, all of chapter 4 could be about reducing litigiousness. But the strategies in that chapter aren't mercenary—they're about honestly meeting families' needs. When you're doing a good job of meeting families' needs, they're much less likely to want to sue you, even if they technically could.

The Spirit of the Law

Again, while the possibility of lawsuits is scary, their existence is well intended. Liability exists to ensure accountability and safety. So while you're doing your due diligence to reduce vulnerability and building relationships to reduce litigiousness, remember to comply with the spirit of the law. In other words, to the best of your ability, be accountable for children's safety and enforce your own highest standards for what is safe.

Your idea of what constitutes safety for young children may differ from the law's (I know mine does), so in addition to living up to legal standards, live up to your own. To me, all the practices described in chapter 3 are about making children safer in the long term—helping them assess risks, learn their own limits, recover from injuries. I know that if anything serious ever happened to a child on my watch, I could honestly say, "I am doing my absolute best to ensure the safety of the children I care for." Make sure you can say the same.

To that end, make sure your practices follow high ethical standards. As Holly Elissa Bruno and Tom Copeland, authors of *Managing Legal Risks in Early Childhood Programs*, write, "Making decisions that are legal *and* ethical is your best protection against a lawsuit" (Bruno and Copeland 2012). So take a close look at NAEYC's *Code of Ethical Conduct and Statement of Commitment* along with your colleagues and figure out how its principles relate to your practice.[2]

Accident Reports and Why They Are the Best Thing Ever

Your school might call them "accident reports," "incident reports," "injury reports," or something else, but you know the thing I mean: those forms you fill out when someone gets hurt and that the family has to sign at pickup time. It's easy to think of them as just an annoying hoop to jump through, but I urge you to give accident reports some respect, because they address every aspect of dealing with liability.

- **Accident reports reduce vulnerability to lawsuits.** They are records you keep, in case anything comes up later, of exactly what happened and what the school did in response; they are also tangible demonstrations of your level of responsibility.

- **Accident reports reduce litigiousness.** By communicating clearly about incidents, accident reports build trust with families, who see them and know that you are taking their children's safety seriously.

- **Accident reports are a tool for accountability.** Or at least, they can be, if you use them proactively to promote safety. Most schools simply collect accident reports in children's files and never give them a second thought, but they can be so much more useful than that. Collect your accident reports and review them periodically, looking for patterns—you might see something habitually going wrong that can be addressed. Lots of head injuries on the slide this month? Maybe there needs to be a new rule for the slide. Lots of crashes on the bikes lately? Maybe the three-year-olds don't yet have the gross-motor skills for bikes and need to wait

---

2   The very first principle in NAEYC's *Code of Ethical Conduct and Statement of Commitment* is "Above all, we shall not harm children." Astute readers might ask, "Aren't we talking about allowing harm to come to children? Letting them get injured? Isn't that a violation of that principle?" These are fair questions, but no, I don't think what we're talking about violates NAEYC's code. Yes, injury is a type of harm, but I see harm as a lot broader than just physical injury. Injury is a universal experience; the skills to recover from injury, sadly, are not. The approaches in this book build the skills that will help children reduce the harm throughout their lives.

a bit. Lots of hair pulling in the block area? Maybe it's time to think about why there are so many conflicts about blocks. Reviewing accident reports can give you a window into children's needs. You can be accountable for children's safety by paying attention to what accident reports tell you.

Building a Culture of Resilience

Even the scary topics of licensing and liability connect to the culture you are building at your school—the shared values, expectations, and practices you create around resilience. When you share the value of resilience, that leads to certain shared expectations: that children will learn in physical ways and naturally take physical risks, and that children will sometimes get injured. Sharing these expectations will help everyone meet the inevitable childhood injuries with equanimity, rather than anger and mistrust.

We can expect that adults who care about children—teachers, licensing consultants, families—will sometimes see different situations differently. We can expect that families will sometimes get upset in response to injuries. You can create practices that address those expectations. Commit yourself to seeking what is best for children and families. Adhere to best practices and to the law. Communicate and build relationships in your practice. Build a culture at your school around children's resilience, and you will not only serve children's interests but also protect your own.

~ 7 ~

Closing Reflections

Resilience isn't the only part of my teaching practice. It's not even the most important part of my teaching practice. Many of you, I imagine, feel the same.

When I think of the perspectives that are core to my teaching, I think of constructivism—letting learning happen through children's self-directed exploratory play. I think of the importance of social development and helping a group of children become a caring, mutually supportive community. I think of looking for learning opportunities in real-life events.

When I remember curriculum I've been especially proud of, I think of the time one of our classroom's pets, Racecar the Rat, died unexpectedly, and the children spent a week planning a memorial service, full of art and songs and heartfelt words. I think of the time a class's interest in *There's a Nightmare in My Closet* led to a months-long exploration of scary stories, in which the children really pushed themselves to explore feeling scared and helping one another be brave. I think of the time a class's interest in the story behind Martin Luther King Day led to a deep exploration of the ways those children knew how to be fair and share and help one another (I still remember three-year-old Anya running up to me shouting, "Jarrod, Jarrod, Tony helped Julia when he let her take a turn on the slide! He was helping, just like Dr. King said!").

When I remember children whose learning and development I can really say I supported, I think of Pat. He cried from the start of naptime all the way until pickup every day for a month, but I helped him gradually see the good parts of school, until he was sad to leave at the end of every day. I think of Brian, who at the start of the year would yell in frustration anytime another child got within three feet of his blocks, but who by spring could be found walking up to friends and saying, "I'm going to start building a castle. Who wants to build a castle with me?" I think of Rose, who was so desperate to always be in control that she once peed in my lap on purpose just to show me I wasn't the boss of her, but by the end of the year was relaxed and flexible in school routines.

Those are all powerful teaching memories of mine that aren't about building resilience. Or then again, are they? The funeral for Racecar the Rat was all about children helping each other bounce back from the sadness of his death. Scary Story Club helped children learn to embrace "negative" feelings like fear and find out how to make themselves feel better. Pat and Brian and Rose and a hundred others learned how to take sad, scary, painful experiences and control them, make active choices, meet their own needs, and recover. These aren't memories of how I helped children get up again after a bump or a scrape; they're about how our work on bumps and scrapes facilitated other kinds of learning. And these other learning experiences undoubtedly helped when there were bumps and scrapes.

Resilience doesn't have to be the most important part of your practice. But it's a value that can touch all the other parts of your practice. Whatever it is that is the core of what you are teaching children, resilience can help.

So what are the craziest stunts you've seen children pull?

I've seen a child hang upside down from the monkey bars by her knees and try to touch the ground.

I've seen a child climb up the slide, climb over the bar at the top, stand on top of the bar, and stand up straight in the air before jumping down.

I've seen two children purposefully knock their foreheads into each other, hard, just to see what would happen.

I've seen a child throw large rocks straight up in the air.

I've seen any number of children jump out of trees, run headlong into each other, crash bikes into walls.

I once saw a child try to jump from the top of the climber holding an umbrella as a parachute, just like a cartoon. (Fortunately I got there in time.)

Why do children do this stuff? Why do they put their own bodies in harm's way? I've come to the conclusion that if these behaviors didn't provide a net benefit, our species would have killed itself off long ago. In fact, considering the potential negative outcomes, the rewards of these behaviors must be really significant.

It only takes a moment of thought to come up with those rewards, because the learning children accomplish through physical risks is tremendous. Children learn how to move their bodies through their environment without bumping into things—a skill that is only built through trial and error. They learn what their bodies are capable of and how their bodies can affect the world around them, giving them a sense of efficacy and power and control. They learn how to keep themselves safe, and how safe the world is (or isn't). They learn to try things out and to persevere if something doesn't go right the first time. They learn to solve problems in the real world, using concentration and attention. They learn that their curiosity can be rewarded as they try out new things. They learn the principles of cause and effect and how to deal with effects that they cause. They learn to communicate about their experiences and ideas and that it's important to cooperate to get anything really exciting done. They learn self-regulation, confidence, and courage. They learn to recover when something goes wrong.

And while children's physical play provides a great deal of learning, it allows for something else equally valuable. Physical play is a way to have adventures. It's a way to experience challenges and the pleasure of overcoming them. It's a time to feel *joy*. Those are vital parts of childhood, just as much as learning is.

All of these are benefits children experience from physical play, "risky" or not—and resilience is the key to all of it. Because whether or not a child is taking crazy risks, he will fall down, he will get bumps and scrapes, he will feel frustrated and scared and upset. With our help, children can build the resilience necessary to shake off those experiences and jump back on that horse, ready to keep experiencing the learning and adventures and joy that come from physical play.

What physical memories do you have from your own childhood? I told you some of mine back at the start of this book. What did you do with your body that made you feel joy and adventure? What did you do that helped you learn something? What did you do that felt like frustration, disappointment, injury? Most of all, what experiences did you have that you want to pass on to the children you care for? What opportunities did you miss that you want to make sure they get in on? Bumps and scrapes are inevitable; the question is, what will come with the bumps and scrapes?

Whatever you want the children you care for to get out of their physical lives, resilience will be a part of it. Learning from mistakes, shaking off upsets, feeling ready to give something a try—resilience gives children access to the best that physical play can offer.

As you—and, ideally, the teachers you work with—put practices in place to help support children in building their resilience, you're not only building resilience in a particular child or group of children; you're also building a culture of resilience. The specifics of that culture will be different for each classroom, for each program, for each school, for each community. But whatever the practices, every culture of resilience will share some beliefs: that physical play and learning are important, that risk comes with rewards, that adults must commit themselves to children's needs. Moreover, a culture of resilience builds on the idea that learning is ongoing for everyone—children, families, teachers—and that taking risks in order to learn and grow is a worthwhile and necessary process at all ages. While it's not necessarily easy, we can do it if we build resilience—not only in children but also in ourselves.

All of this, though, is simply an attempt to answer the final reflection question of this book: *What will we give to children?* My goal is to give children the experiences of learning and joy, challenge and triumph, and the ability to enter the world, with all its challenges and obstacles and setbacks, in the most positive way possible.

What will you give them?

~ Appendix A ~

Sample "Workshop on Resilience" Outline for Families

As discussed in chapter 4, you can work towards a culture of resilience in your program by inviting families to discuss the issue. A workshop can be a great context for both discussion and education. Use or adapt this outline to host a productive conversation with families about resilience.

20 min	**Icebreaker conversation**	What are dangerous things you remember doing as a child? How did you feel when you were doing those things? Do your children have similar experiences today? How do you feel about your child's experiences with danger?
5 min	**Brainstorm**	What is resilience? Why is resilience important? (Be sure to have your own ideas on this formulated so that you can be part of the conversation.)
5 min	**Building resilience in children**	Briefly describe the importance to children's development of learning through trial and error, support in overcoming negative emotions, finding opportunities to take risks, and adults letting children try their own ideas.
25 min	**Injuries**	What are some injuries your child has gotten recently? How do you feel when your child gets injured? How do you usually respond? Do you think your usual response helps build resilience?

Discuss Jarrod's steps for responding to injuries (p. 58): Wait, Wait Again, Communicate, and Empower. Give examples or try some role playing.

30 min	**Risk**

What are some physical risks your child has taken recently? How do you feel when your child takes risks? How do you usually respond? Do you think your usual response helps build resilience?

Discuss Jarrod's steps for responding to risky behaviors from chapter 3 (p. 40): Trust, Observe, Evaluate, and Act, using the least restrictive action, such as providing information, encouraging memory and foresight, and engaging reflection and self-knowledge. Give examples or try some role playing.

5 min	**Wrap-up**

Describe how resilience connects with your program and curriculum.

~ Appendix B ~

Further Reading and Resources

Resilience

Ginsburg, Kenneth R. 2015. *Building Resilience in Children and Teens: Giving Kids Roots and Wings*, 3rd ed. Elk Grove Village, IL: American Academy of Pediatrics.

Reivich, Karen and Andrew Shattle. 2002. *The Resilience Factor: 7 Keys to Finding Your Inner Strength and Overcoming Life's Hurdles.* New York: Broadway Books.

Tough, Paul. 2013. *How Children Succeed: Grit, Curiosity, and the Hidden Power of Character.* New York: Haughton Mifflin Harcourt.

"Dangerous" Play

Carlson, Frances M. 2012. "Rough Play: One of the Most Challenging Behaviors." *Teaching Young Children* 5 (4): 18–25.

DeBenedet, Anthony T., and Lawrence J. Cohen. 2010. *The Art of Roughhousing: Good Old-Fashioned Horseplay and Why Every Kid Needs It.* Philadelphia: Quirk Books.

Kirn, Walter. 2007. "Boys Gone Mild." *New York Times*, June 3.

Solly, Kathryn. 2015. *Risk, Challenge and Adventure in the Early Years: A Practical Guide to Exploring and Extending Learning Outdoors.* New York: Routledge.

Tulley, Gever, and Julie Spiegler. 2009. *50 Dangerous Things (You Should Let Your Children Do).* New York: New American Library.

Physical Development and Beyond

Healy, Michelle. 2012. "Keep Recess in Play, Pediatricians Urge." *USA Today*, December 31.

Jensen, Eric. 2000. "Moving with the Brain in Mind." *Educational Leadership* 58 (3): 34–37.

Murray, Robert, and Catherine Ramstetter. 2013. "The Crucial Role of Recess in School." *Pediatrics* 131 (1): 183–88.

Pica, Rae. 1997. "Beyond Physical Development: Why Young Children Need to Move." *Young Children* 52 (6): 4–11.

Sandseter, Ellen Beate Hansen, and Leif Edward Ottesen Kennair. 2011. "Children's Risky Play from an Evolutionary Perspective: The Anti-Phobic Effects of Thrilling Experiences." *Evolutionary Psychology* 9 (2): 257–284.

Stephenson, Alison. 2003. "Physical Risk-taking: Dangerous or Endangered?" *Early Years: An International Research Journal* 23 (1): 35–43.

Sensory Needs

Cross, Aerial. 2009. *Ants in Their Pants: Teaching Children Who Must Move to Learn*. St. Paul: Redleaf Press.

Kranowitz, Carol Stock. 2006. *The Out-of-Sync Child: Recognizing and Coping with Sensory Processing Disorder*. New York: Penguin.

Kranowitz, Carol Stock. 2006. *The Out-of-Sync Child Has Fun: Activities for Kids with Sensory Processing Disorder*. New York: Penguin.

Health and Safety

Mogel, Wendy. 2001. *The Blessings of a Skinned Knee: Using Jewish Teachings to Raise Self-Reliant Children*. New York: Penguin.

Olsen, Heather M., Susan D. Hudson, and Donna Thompson. 2016. *SAFE and Fun Playgrounds: A Handbook*. St. Paul: Redleaf Press.

Rosin, Hanna. 2014. "The Overprotected Kid." *The Atlantic*, March 19.

Physical Environment (Gross Motor)

Curtis, Deb, and Margie Carter. 2011. *Reflecting Children's Lives: A Handbook for Planning a Child-Centered Curriculum*, 2nd ed. St. Paul: Redleaf Press.

Hosking, Wes. 2013. "Hay Bales and Milk Crates Better for Creative Play Than Conventional School Playgrounds." *Herald Sun*, December 9.

Skulski, Jennifer K. 2007. "Designing for Inclusive Play: Applying the Principles of Universal Design to the Playground." Bloomington, IN: National Center on Accessibility, Indiana University-Bloomington. www.ncaonline. org/resources/articles/playground-universaldesign.shtml.

Sobel, David. 2016. *Nature Preschools and Forest Kindergartens: The Handbook for Outdoor Learning.* St. Paul: Redleaf Press.

www.InclusivePlaygrounds.org.

Working with Families

Bruno, Holly Elissa. 2012. "Family-Friendly Practices." *Teaching Young Children* 5 (5): 6–7.

Keyser, Janis. 2006. *From Parents to Partners: Building a Family-Centered Early Childhood Program.* St. Paul: Redleaf Press

Powers, Julie. 2016. *Parent Engagement in Early Learning: Strategies for Working with Families,* 2nd ed. St. Paul: Redleaf Press.

Schweikert, Gigi. 2012. *Winning Ways for Early Childhood Professionals: Partnering with Families.* St. Paul: Redleaf Press.

Teacher Development and School Change

Bruno, Holly Elissa. 2015. *The Comfort of Little Things: An Educator's Guide to Second Chances.* St. Paul, Redleaf Press.

Curtis, Deb, and Margie Carter. 2011. *Reflecting Children's Lives: A Handbook for Planning Your Child-Centered Curriculum,* 2nd ed. St. Paul: Redleaf Press.

Evans, Robert. 1996. *The Human Side of School Change: Reform, Resistance, and the Real-Life Problems of Innovation.* San Francisco: Jossey-Bass.

Romeo, Nick. 2014. "Are Great Teachers Born or Made?" *The Atlantic,* August 6.

Licensing and Liability

Bruno, Holly Elissa, and Tom Copeland. 2012. *Managing Legal Risks in Early Childhood Programs: How to Prevent Flare-Ups from Becoming Lawsuits.* St. Paul: Redleaf Press.

Ethics

Feeney, Stephanie, and Nancy K. Freeman. 2012. *Ethics and the Early Childhood Educator: Using the NAEYC Code,* 2nd ed. Washington, DC: NAEYC.

Fennimore, Beatrice S. 2014. *Standing Up for Something Every Day: Ethics and Justice in Early Childhood Classrooms.* New York: Teachers College Press.

National Association for the Education of Young Children. 2005. *Code of Ethical Conduct and Statement of Commitment.* Washington, DC: NAEYC.

~ Notes ~

Chapter 1

page 11, children in today's culture in the United States experience much less unsupervised play: Esther Entin, "All Work and No Play: Why Your Kids Are More Anxious, Depressed," *Atlantic*, October 12, 2011, www.theatlantic.com/health/archive/2011/10/all-work-and-no-play-why-your-kids-are-more-anxious-depressed/246422.

page 12, violent crimes have fallen by more than half since the early 1990s: Justin Wolfers, "Perceptions Haven't Caught Up to Decline in Crime," *New York Times*, September 16, 2014, www.nytimes.com/2014/09/17/upshot/perceptions-havent-caught-up-to-decline-in-crime.html?_r=0.

page 12, crime against children committed by strangers is astonishingly rare: Lenore Skenazy, "Crime Statistics," *Free-Range Kids*, accessed December 26, 2015, www.freerangekids.com/crime-statistics.

Chapter 2

page 18, a complete lack of germs isn't healthy for children: Steve Mirsky, "Can It Be Bad to Be Too Clean? The Hygiene Hypothesis," *Scientific American*, April 6, 2011, www.scientificamerican.com/podcast/episode/can-it-be-bad-to-be-too-clean-the-h-11-04-06; Michael Specter, "Germs Are Us: Bacteria Make Us Sick. Do They Also Keep Us Alive?" *New Yorker*, October 22, 2012, www.newyorker.com/magazine/2012/10/22/germs-are-us.

page 18, babies who grow up in houses with pets: Amina Khan, "Dog and Cats Help Babies' Health, Study Finds," *Los Angeles Times*, July 9, 2012, http://articles.latimes.com/2012/jul/09/science/la-sci-dogs-cats-babies-health-20120709.

page 18, the Royal Society for the Prevention of Accidents has spent the last: Royal Society for the Prevention of Accidents, *RoSPA Review 09:10*, accessed December 26, 2015, www.rospa.com/RoSPAWeb/docs/about/annual-review/past-years/review2010.pdf.

page 20, tens of thousands of Americans die in car accidents every year: National Highway Traffic Safety Administration, "U.S. Department of Transportation Announces Decline in Traffic Fatalities in 2013," December 19, 2014, www.nhtsa.gov/About+NHTSA/Press+Releases/2014/traffic-deaths-decline-in-2013.

page 21, US cities are the safest they've been in decades: Justin Wolfers, "Perceptions Haven't Caught Up to Decline in Crime," *New York Times*, September 16, 2014, www.nytimes.com/2014/09/17/upshot/perceptions-havent-caught-up-to-decline-in-crime.html?_r=0.

page 23, humans are, by and large, astonishingly bad at risk assessment: Alison George, "What Gamblers and Weather Forecasters Can Teach Us about Risk: An Interview with the Creator of the 'Risk Quotient' Intelligence Scale," Slate, May 22, 2012, www.slate.com/articles/health_and_science/new_scientist/2012/05/risk_intelligence_how_gamblers_and_weather_forecasters_assess_probabilities_.html.

page 24, children's bodies heal much faster than adults': Luisa Dillner, "How Did a Baby Survive an Air Crash That Killed Over 100 People?" *Guardian*, July 15, 2003, www.theguardian.com/lifeandstyle/2003/jul/15/healthandwellbeing.health1.

page 27, deaths from car accidents have fallen dramatically: Matthew L. Wald, "Tougher Seat Belt Laws Save Lives, Study Finds," *New York Times*, November 17, 2003, www.nytimes.com/2003/11/17/us/tougher-seat-belt-laws-save-lives-study-finds.html; Centers for Disease Control, "Condom Distribution as a Structural Level Intervention," last updated June 11, 2015, www.cdc.gov/hiv/prevention/programs/condoms.

Chapter 3

page 37, "If you have no bloody owies," he says: Tom Hobson, "The Right Number of Bloody Owies," *Teacher Tom* (blog), September 25, 2014, http://teachertomsblog.blogspot.com/2014/09/the-right-number-of-bloody-owies.html.

Chapter 4

page 68, "Families are of primary importance in children's development": The National Association for the Education of Young Children (NAEYC), *Code of Ethical Conduct and Statement of Commitment*, revised April 2005, www.naeyc.org/files/naeyc/file/positions/PSETH05.pdf.

Chapter 5

page 95, "Though we exalt [change] in principle," he writes: Robert Evans, *The Human Side of School Change: Reform, Resistance, and the Real-Life Problems of Innovation* (San Francisco: Jossey-Bass, 2001), 23.

page 96, change "provokes loss, challenges competence, creates confusion, and causes conflict": Evans, *The Human Side of School Change*, 19.

page 96, "Reformers who press staff to innovate have already assimilated": Evans, *The Human Side of School Change*, 21.

Chapter 6

page 119, "Making decisions that are legal *and* ethical": Holly Elissa Bruno and Tom Copeland, *Managing Legal Risks in Early Childhood Programs* (Saint Paul, MN: Redleaf Press, 2012), 21.

~ Index ~